Perfectly Ordinary

Perfectly Ordinary

In search of healthy church leadership

Marcus Throup

CANTERBURY
PRESS
Norwich

© Marcus Throup 2024

First published in 2024 by the Canterbury Press Norwich
Editorial office
3rd Floor, Invicta House
110 Golden Lane,
London EC1Y 0TG, UK

www.canterburypress.co.uk

Canterbury Press is an imprint of Hymns Ancient & Modern Ltd
(a registered charity)

Hymns Ancient & Modern® is a registered trademark of
Hymns Ancient & Modern Ltd
13A Hellesdon Park Road, Norwich,
Norfolk NR6 5DR, UK

British Library Cataloguing in Publication data

A catalogue record for this book is available
from the British Library

ISBN: 978 1 78622 585 6

Typeset by Regent Typesetting

Contents

For Mum

Preface

Confronted with a seemingly unending stream of bad news stories concerning church leaders, it was more a sense of compulsion than design that birthed this book. I was not planning on writing it, but the subject matter has demanded my attention, forcing other stuff onto the back burner. When church leadership goes wrong this is what happens. The schedule goes out the window, plans are kicked into touch and, forced into 'crisis mode', our focus inevitably shifts. In 25 years of ministry, I have witnessed the pain when it has fallen apart for clergy colleagues, and when churches have tailspun into the mire of scandal. At various times, in small ways I have tried to support people affected by church-based abuse and the harmful ripple effect of the social media circus. The reader can be assured that this volume has been written in consultation with some of these courageous people.

Primarily, this book is offered as a word for people called to positions of responsibility and leadership in the church and for those who are currently discerning such a call. First and foremost, this is a book about Christian leadership and the type of leaders we so desperately need. My own context is that of the Anglican Communion and specifically the Church of England. Institutionally, we are struggling with heavy burdens. Our safeguarding failures have become the subject of documentaries and dramatizations. Our historic failure to embrace people from all cultures and ethnicities is the subject of books, internal inquiries, reports and redress schemes. This demoralizing state of disrepair is as much the result of successive failures of leadership on the macro stage as it is of the abuse, bullying and deference culture that has often plagued our churches on a local level. Collectively, we need to do much better and, in its own way, this book calls for a 'reset' in how we go about the vital task and privilege that is Christian leadership.

In relation to the scandals emerging in churches and Christian organizations across all denominations, whether here at home or overseas, certain patterns can be identified. Exceptionally gifted leaders on meteoric trajectories come crashing down to earth when moral failures and unresolved personal issues culminate in bullying behaviours that are unchristian, ungodly and – in a word – abusive. In such cases exaggerated cultures of deference have sometimes shielded celebrity leaders from whistleblowers and investigative processes. This is similarly true of the stomach-churning accounts of predators hiding in plain sight, where position and status become both the levers and the subterfuge for intentional and systemic abuse carried out over lengthy periods of time. When Christian leaders are put on a pedestal and regarded as superhuman or quasi-angelic beings, the right conditions are created for wrong things to happen and to keep on happening. It is increasingly clear that clericalism goes hand in hand with church-based abuse.

For the avoidance of doubt, this is not some holier-than-thou crusade or self-righteous exercise in finger pointing. Far be it from me to claim some supposed moral high ground. Though in some chapters there is an element of what I would like to think of as *prophetic heckling*, the point of this is merely to get the point across. We simply have to call out unhealthy leadership models if we want to see a healthier church. That said, names that have been named elsewhere need not be named here. While it is of course vitally important to call out and report any and all forms of abuse, there is little merit in naming and shaming in a publication such as this. In any case, our task is not really about scrutinizing or revisiting the specific errors of particular individuals – pastors, priests or bishops who have hit the headlines for all the wrong reasons – rather, it is about addressing the collective failure of our churches in relation to a certain leader *type*. Thus, Chapters 1–3 cover some reasonably common scenarios and unhealthy leadership models that I have experienced in different regions of the globe, but without naming names. The point is, sadly, that the many scandals that have blown up in Christian circles in decades past and in more recent times can occur anywhere.

Similarly, though I am an Anglican the critique articulated herein is not limited to a specific church denomination or expression of the Christian faith. The problems to be explored here are not the exclusive preserve of any single church or para-church organization, and no church or Christian group is immune from the possibility of abusive leadership. Bad eggs who are deceptively *gifted actors* can wheedle their way into positions of power, and gain influence within any church set-up. Thus, in the interests of a constructive approach, this book seeks to identify the hallmarks of unhealthy and abusive leadership cultures, inviting those of us in Christian leadership to take a long hard look at ourselves and to assess risk in our own contexts. Such an approach can then explore a different paradigm of leadership over against unhealthy models, promoting practical measures that will not only help prevent harmful subcultures from taking hold, but will encourage the building of church communities that are more Christ-focused, integral and salubrious.

I make no claim to be saying anything especially new or ground-breaking here. Rather, this book takes its place alongside other recent publications (Chapter 1 note 2). Together this emerging body of literature voices a burgeoning and impassioned plea for church leaders to take a deliberate step back so that going forwards ministry might follow faithfully in the footsteps of Christ. The Gospels make it plain that Jesus valued the people whom others simply failed to notice or else reviled. Nobody is a *nobody*, and the Gospels tell of a Saviour who made time for 'normal' people wherever and whenever he encountered them. Refusing to make ministry about the minister, Jesus prioritized others, particularly the vulnerable and those on the margins. Moreover, the carpenter-Messiah resisted the trappings and temptations of worldly power and renown (cf. Matthew 4). Likewise for those who dare to minister in Jesus' name today, the true path of leadership is one of self-abnegation, simplicity and sincerity. The prerogative has to be the cultivation of a quiet faithfulness in the daily and unchangingly challenging quest for godliness and authentic discipleship. This is a far cry from the pop-star-gospel approach that makes 'me' the centre of 'my' ministry (with emphasis on the 'my'), and tends to attract groupies rather than grow disciples.

Thus, in a world where celebrity worship is increasingly the norm, this book makes an alternative pitch to forgo the allure of the limelight, sidestepping the ever-present snares and cul-de-sacs of ungodly personal ambition in order to pursue *unspectacular* leadership. What we are after is a leadership pattern marked out by a prayerful Jesus-centred approach to life and ministry with healthy and realistic expectations (Chapter 4). As *ordinary leaders* (Chapter 5), the priority is to recognize the value of who we are in Christ and rejoice in the simple life-giving facets of ministry, resisting the urge to compare ourselves to others or judge ourselves according to someone else's yardstick. This in turn raises the question of our pastoring and preaching, and the need for a down-to-earth and wholly unsensational way to communicate (Chapter 6). Something will need to be said about wellbeing – and, indeed, *being* well in an age where ministers face significant pressures and can feel 'pressed on every side' (Chapter 7). Then there is a piece on the importance of place, and how the stewarding of self dovetails with the care of others as we seek to curate safe, life-giving places of grace (Chapter 8). Finally, there comes a word on encouraging the next generation of Christian leaders by deliberately stepping aside to allow others to come forward and build the Kingdom alongside us and in our place (Chapter 9).

As a text written for Christian leaders seeking a healthy leadership model, this work focuses primarily on our role and responsibilities before God and opens by highlighting the dangers of abusive leadership. It begins where I think such a text should begin, in the concrete experience of people who have been on the receiving end of unhealthy Christian leadership, and have had to piece together their lives in the aftermath. Therefore, integrated into Chapter 1 are the voices of those who have suffered and survived church-based spiritual abuse. These are fragments of and insights into people's stories that, sadly, will resonate with the experiences of many survivors from different churches in places across the world. If you are affected by anything you read here and believe that you may have been a victim of church-based abuse, please contact the safeguarding authority within your church or church organization or get in touch with an independent body such as Thirtyone:eight (www. thirtyoneeight.org).

A disclaimer: what is minimally or only implicitly covered here, and would undoubtedly comprise a volume in its own right, is the subject of Christian leaders *themselves* being victims of abuse and bullying. Sadly, it is not uncommon for ministers and other Christian leaders to find themselves on the receiving end of manipulative, bullying and inappropriate behaviour from others – whether these 'others' are other leaders or members of their church congregation or organization. Those who have experienced this know all too well that it can be excruciatingly painful, comprising a genuine threat to one's ministry, wellbeing and livelihood. Once more, if that is something you are currently undergoing or suspect you might be experiencing, please reach out to your safeguarding authority and/or seek support from an independent organization such as Thirtyone:eight.

Finally, this book seeks to confront unhealthy, abusive models of leadership – especially in relation to *spiritual abuse* – and to speak into this troubled and troubling area. My hope is that readers might understand better why things can and do sometimes go wrong in Christian leadership so that together we might seek to unlock a more hopeful Christ-centred way of leading the people of God in our churches and parachurch organizations. For me, as explained in the ensuing chapters, this hope-filled trajectory is the everyday no-frills but fully faithful model of *unspectacular* leadership held by *ordinary* leaders. It strikes me that such an unpretentious, unglamorous *back to basics* sort of leadership will lead to safer, happier, healthier churches filled with the grace of God.

PART I

A widespread leadership problem

I

Calling out spiritually
abusive leadership

If the life of those who are united to Christ is patterned after Christ's humble self-giving love, then a life that consistently fails to demonstrate that pattern, but nevertheless professes or claims his name, bears his name in vain. It misrepresents the character of God. (Mark Stirling)[1]

A sober understanding of sin means we are all implicated, and precludes the Pharisaism that says, 'I thank you, God, that I am not like this abuser' (Luke 18.11). If sin is the common problem of every person, then we are all potential participants in abuse, whether as victims, bystanders, or perpetrators. (Nick Mackison)[2]

This is a book for Christian leaders about Christian leadership. More pointedly, in common with other recent publications, it faces up to the fact that sometimes things can and do go wrong in ministry.[3] Sometimes ministers and church workers get things badly wrong. Whenever and wherever things go wrong in the lives and ministries of Christian leaders and when church workers wrong others, much hurt is caused. Inside and outside the church, unsafe and abusive leadership can take many different forms and might not be obvious. For instance, it can sometimes happen that the behaviour of a well-intentioned and possibly well-loved leader may become unhealthy over time. And without negating the seriousness of the harm it can cause, with certain forms of church-based abuse it is not necessarily the case that abusive behaviour is committed intentionally and knowingly. We should be careful not to assume too much when things go wrong in church.

What is clear, however, is that Christian leaders who strive 'to do Jesus' work in ways that are inconsistent with Jesus' example and teaching' risk falling into a pattern of unhealthy leadership that can slide into *pastoral* or *spiritual abuse*.[4] 'Spiritual abuse' is arguably the most common form of church-based abuse and yet it has reached our radar screens only relatively recently. Our foregrounding of this particular type of abuse reflects the fact that it is less well known and less readily identifiable than other forms. Equally, the focus on spiritual abuse voices a growing conviction that this variety of abuse needs to be taken extremely seriously by church leaders and those who are exploring a vocation to church ministry. Before we come to a fuller exploration of this terminology, along with some possible definitions, a couple of framing considerations must be mentioned.

First, at the heart of spiritual abuse is the question of power and authority: how power and authority are held and exercised by church leaders. Reflecting on the famous Christological passage in Philippians 2.5–11, Mark Stirling infers that Christian leaders receive power in order to engender the growth and flourishing of others through a life patterned on Jesus' humble self-giving. Thus, where leaders hold and use power healthily this bears fruit in the nurturing and empowering of others. Conversely, any use of power 'to get something from others or to defend oneself against the cost of loving others is, by definition, misuse of power'.[5] Spiritual abuse, then, is first and foremost *an abuse of power* – something that disempowers, disenfranchises and ultimately devalues people.

Second, this abuse of power acts on the desire to control both structures and people (not necessarily in that order) within a religious context.[6] To get more granular about it, spiritual abuse involves coercive control, bullying, suppression and emotional blackmail where sacred texts are twisted to become pretexts so that Scripture becomes weaponized against questioning or non-compliant individuals. Typically, spiritually abusive leaders seek to justify or defend their actions by way of misguided appeals to biblical texts and by referencing their personal sense of divine calling or 'anointing'. Ultimately, the manipulative behaviour patterns employed in spiritually abusive leadership are designed to gain and then retain power over a religious organization and the people within it.

As we move deeper into our topic we will try and unpack these themes a little more, but at this point I have to put down my pen and do some listening. This is because I want to avoid an approach that is too *theoretical* when so much of what we are talking about here is gut-wrenchingly *experiential*, being experienced and deeply felt at the human level. To that end an instructive way into the topic of spiritual abuse comes via the words and recollections of survivors. I am grateful to the people who have shared their stories with me and, as we listen to their voices, the following short excerpts provide an indication of how the actions and attitudes of spiritually abusive church workers can impact and damage the lives of disciples of Christ.

'Because of the intimidation tactics of the people in charge and in particular one very influential figure who led a cult-like operation from within the church, I found myself struggling to face the world outside. I had become too anxious to answer the phone and, though I didn't know it at the time, I was going through a nervous breakdown. It took several years of therapy to recover.'

'A kind of religious mania had overtaken the community where leaders were revered unhealthily as modern-day prophets. A controlling "heavy-shepherding" approach had become the normative leadership paradigm. Churchgoers were pressured to sell up and move into the village so as to be "close to the centre". While wealthy professionals were taken under the wing and treated as insiders, others seemed to be less important – disposable even. Every member of the church was expected to spring into action as and when the leaders clicked their fingers, and in some cases folks were guilt-tripped into doing full-time work for the church for free.'

'It was bad enough for me and I became very ill, but thankfully I got out. I felt really sorry for some of the lovely people in the congregation who just didn't deserve to be treated like that. There was a woman whose long-term sickness was unresponsive to the prayers of the pastors. The fact that she continued unwell was explained away on the basis of a "lack of faith", "rebellion" and even "demons". Poor woman. People tried to get out but were emotionally and spiritually blackmailed into staying.'

It is deeply sad and painfully ironic that some people's experience of the church – often referred to as a 'hospital for sinners' – has proved to be so wounding and lastingly harmful.[7] Every form of abuse – physical, sexual, emotional, spiritual – is serious and comprises an unchristian affront to the Jesus way. On the surface of things this truth is so plainly obvious, so utterly self-evident that in part it maybe explains – though in no way justifies – why abusers have sometimes gone under the radar in churches. Often, church (i.e. the church building) is thought of as 'the house of God', a *sacred* place. For unsuspecting parishioners the notion of something untoward happening within the hallowed walls of their local church would be simply unconscionable. By the same token, until recently clergy and other church workers have enjoyed automatic and almost unqualified trust, being universally regarded as upstanding societal figureheads, 'pillars of the community' who are 'above all suspicion'.

Theology recognizes the tension between life in the 'now' and the eschatological 'not yet'. It recognizes that the Christian hope of future restoration and regeneration can seemingly be frustrated by both moral failings and wicked actions in the present. Though such evil will ultimately be overcome as Christ is revealed in the fullness of time, this end goal stands in tension with the current state of play in a broken world. So too in relation to ecclesiology – that is, the character and governance of the church – we find certain tensions. Just as the Christian is both justified in Christ and yet continues sinful, so, says Luther, is the church on earth.[8] A careful reading of the New Testament cautions against naïve, sentimental and unrealistically rosy understandings of the church. This side of glory, the *ecclesia* is as much a compendium of sinners as it is a communion of saints. Notwithstanding all the life-giving, life-transforming, life-renewing, genuinely good stuff that we can expect to find in churches, from time to time things go wrong.

Often, when things go wrong in churches and parachurch organizations it is, at one level, because people are people. Experientially we know that people who are capable of doing good things are simultaneously liable to get it wrong and to fail in other ways. This is just as true of Christian leaders as it is of anyone else. Because people are people, every single day presents opportunities to make good or bad decisions and no-one is immune from getting things wrong. However, in Christian leadership, alarm bells sound when we ourselves, or leaders within our teams, fall into unhealthy patterns and repeated behaviours that are *harmful* to others. Getting it wrong is one thing, but it is quite another to fall into and perpetuate the damaging patterns of spiritual abuse that wrong others. Healthy leadership ensures that checks and balances and the right sort of accountability are in place – unhealthy leadership tends to lack or downplay these mechanisms that can prevent people from inculcating unhealthy patterns of control, manipulation and bullying behaviour.

Whereas the vast majority of Christian leaders are well-intentioned, trustworthy, committed and caring custodians of community, there are exceptions to the rule. Pointedly, not everyone who purports to be a Christian leader is led by Christ: 'Why do you call me "Lord, Lord", and do not do what I tell you?' (Luke 6.46). On occasion, when things go wrong in church it is because individuals elevated to positions of trust show themselves to be entirely unworthy of that trust. To put it another way, occasionally things go wrong in churches because people are not the people they purport to be. But this is not just about those heinous, infamous and even psychopathic abusers who make the headlines for all the wrong reasons. In regard to spiritually abusive leaders, a well-meaning person might take on the role of pastor, minister or church worker who turns out to be psychologically unfit or spiritually unprepared for that role. Their intentions may be good but unresolved underlying issues, emotional blind spots and psychological insecurities impact negatively on their leadership in a way that spills out so as to become corrosive and harmful to others. But abuse is *abuse* irrespective of intentionality. The abuser who is blinkered by a warped and myopic self-understanding and is to some extent unaware of the impact that their abusive behaviour has on others is nonetheless responsible for damage done to victims and must be held to account.[9]

To circle back round to terminology, our brief excerpts from survivors provide snapshots of what is increasingly referred to as 'spiritual abuse'. Although the phrase 'spiritual abuse' began to feature in the North American context in the 1990s, the term has gained more widespread traction only in recent years.[10] As mentioned above, we are talking first and foremost about an abuse of power and the tendency to control others. Once more, spiritual abuse is characterized by a manipulative form of bullying that takes place within a religious context, 'a religious variant of emotional and psychological domination'.[11] In their landmark study, Oakley and Humphreys define spiritual abuse as 'a form of emotional and psychological abuse … characterized by a systematic pattern of coercive and controlling behaviour in a religious context'.[12]

While spiritual abuse shares similarities with other forms of abuse, the *religious* dimension highlighted in these definitions is what categorizes and signposts this type of abuse. As Samuel Fernandez puts it, 'the fact that spiritual abuse involves the name of God, means that it hurts people on their religious level'.[13] This statement is patently true, but if it sounds a little abstract or hypothetical, the following testimony from a survivor of spiritual abuse sheds light on what this means in practice:

'The most devastating aspect for me was the travesty of turning "my" scriptures on their head … All I'd known to be good, right and true about my Lord and central to my being was turned on its head to cause harm and hurt. I knew in my heart that this was utterly wrong, so I experienced this as deeply confusing, promoted as it was by the leadership of the church. The inner conflict and self-doubt was mentally destructive. My deep faith, central to my life and being, was under a confusing assault from the very people I knew should be speaking grace, truth and love in accordance with the scriptures.'

To pick up and run with these words, rather than speaking 'grace, truth and love in accordance with the scriptures' we note once again that spiritually abusive leaders tend to adopt a 'divine position' and exhibit the propensity to 'exercise control through a misuse of Scripture'.[14] Adapting a memorable phrase from Mark Stirling, we could say that this sort of behaviour *misuses Jesus' name in non-Jesus ways*.[15] Where domineering and authoritarian leaders misuse their power to build themselves up and knock others down, claims of a special prophetic anointing shield against any potential or de facto challenge. Whether calculated or knee-jerk, proof-texting from Scripture as a strategy to back up bullying behaviour disempowers and alienates the congregation. In such situations it is easy to see how Christians brought up to respect authority and seek guidance from ministers can become putty in the hands of a spiritual abuser. All too often the typically unquestioning deference culture that is commonplace in many churches provides the perfect backdrop for spiritually abusive leaders who claim to speak with divine authority but in true pharisaic fashion lay heavy burdens on the shoulders of the people (Matthew 23.4). We shall have more to say about those dangerously toxic subcultures of deference in Chapter 2.

To reinforce an earlier point, when considering spiritually abusive Christian leaders we must not assume that every scenario is the same or that the personalities involved are somehow monochrome. In his astute volume *Abus Spirituels*, French pastor and psychologist Jacques Poujol identifies three types of abusive religious figurehead, differentiating these on account of motive and intentionality.[16] These range from the psychologically insecure Christian leader, who may be somewhat unaware of their bullying behaviour and its damaging effects, to the veritable wolf in sheep's clothing, whose abuse is premeditated, calculating, covert and frighteningly systematic in character (cf. Acts 20.29). It is Poujol's threefold schematization to which we will now turn in order to get a better handle on the taxonomy of spiritually abusive leaders and to investigate what might underlie their manipulative manoeuvrings and harmful modus operandi.

What is it that characterizes spiritually abusive leaders?

Poujol puts his finger on three types of spiritually abusive leader – what he calls the *overprotective leader*, the *egocentric leader* and the *perverse narcissistic Christian leader*.[17] Taking these in turn, in scenarios like those described by survivors in the excerpts above, overprotective leaders insist on strong-arming church members, becoming inappropriately directive about their life choices and censuring their decision-making. Believing themselves to know what is best for others, overprotective leaders offer pseudo-spiritual *guidance* that in reality denies any element of choice and amounts to inappropriate interference. Such leaders insist on mollycoddling and meddling in the lives of church members in a way that restricts their autonomy, their freedom and ultimately their personhood. As a chess player casts their hand upon the head of a pawn to usher it from square to square, so the coercive controller predetermines the moves that church members are to make in a calculated and intentional way.

Nowadays *heavy shepherding* is a well-worn phrase but it remains useful, for here the instinct is to 'hem in' and control the flock. Poujol observes that where a church member resists such spiritual suffocation and controlling paternalism, the overprotective leader is likely to show their true colours and domineering tendency, excoriating the 'rebellious' and 'ungrateful' individual.[18] We might observe that it is at this point in particular where victims of such abuse find themselves stuck between a rock and a hard place. On the one hand they may feel a sense of guilt at having challenged the 'anointed' leader, and this could translate into more obsequious behaviour and attempts to win back the approval of the abuser. Simultaneously, however, the *flight* instinct is likely to kick in so that the person on the end of the bullying is torn between going deeper into the relationship with the abuser and getting out altogether – though the latter, as described in the recollections from survivors above, can be notoriously difficult to achieve in practice.[19]

Taking a step back, we are well within our rights to ask what in heaven's name is going on with the overprotective leader who stifles and stultifies the spiritual and emotional lives of their congregation. Psychology teaches us that controlling behaviours and overactive desires to protect and 'mother' others to the nth degree are often rooted in some form of negative childhood experience.[20] In reality, the overprotective and dictatorial leader is likely to be someone who suffers from a deficit of self-esteem. Frequently, the existence of some unaddressed trauma or series of events in early life can cause an individual to transfer or project their neediness onto others and to create a kind of co-dependent relationship.[21] There is a multilayered irony herein, namely that in striving on the surface of it to help others, such leaders do more harm than good when they themselves are in need of help and even protection from themselves.

Mutatis mutandis the same is true of the self-obsessed and self-promoting *egocentric* leader. While such figures are outwardly bold and ostensibly confident performers, remove the mask and *egocentrics* are likely to have low self-esteem, leaning heavily on others in order to build themselves up. The local church or parachurch organization becomes the place where egocentric leaders can tend what Poujol calls the 'narcissistic wound'.[22] Once more, some past unresolved issue(s) or negatively formative experience(s) leaves them profoundly insecure, desperate for attention, affirmation, acceptance and affection. Whether it be well disguised or thinly veiled, such leaders are exaggeratedly self-centred and instinctively self-referential. In a nutshell, everything they do screams, 'Me, me, me!'

On the pretence of making and growing disciples of Jesus Christ, abusive egocentrics can set up their own micro kingdoms, grooming sycophantic serfs who are expected to be unflinchingly loyal to their *king*. 'Insiders' will get in line and form part of the unquestioning entourage. Those who dare to question, doubt or in some way resist are talked down, outmanoeuvred, circumnavigated, ousted or else ignored and alienated, becoming 'outsiders'.[23] Entirely consumed by their disproportionate and disordered need for recognition, egocentrics who long for the limelight can be surprisingly unreflective and actively engage in censorship. In some cases these leaders can be virtually blind to the detrimental and damaging effects that their manipulative and game-playing antics can have on others.[24] We will say more about these egocentrics when we delve into the domain of *showmen* leaders in Chapter 3.

Turning to Poujol's third and final category, whereas overprotective leaders and egocentric leaders might be described as *problematic people* who have the potential to do great harm, in the case of the *perverse narcissist* we are talking about a dangerous psychopathic *personality*.[25] By and large, the latter are devious individuals who commit abuse intentionally in pre-planned or opportunistic actions. When discovered, such persons can end up behind bars. The abusive behaviour of the *perverse narcissist* can take several forms, often combined – spiritual, sexual, physical, etc. To this group of abusers belong those sickening stories of systematic abuse aired in documentaries or recreated in stomach-churning TV dramatizations. Whereas overprotective and egocentric leaders can experience contrition, seek help and potentially change their ways, this is not generally thought to be the case with predatory psychopathic personalities. Instead, a total absence of empathy for others leads to morally perverse abusive patterns that are as fixed as the perpetrator is devoid of remorse.[26]

At one level, then, this threefold schematization helps us to see that there is a clear difference between the psychopathic abuser who loves to play God and uses religion to cynically camouflage intentionally abusive and predatory behaviours, and the overprotective leader who genuinely believes that their conduct is above reproach and in the best interests of 'the flock'. Thus, in relation specifically to spiritual abuse, Oakley and Humphreys point out that the fairly liberal use of Jesus' well-known saying about wolves in sheep's clothing is not always on the money.[27] Once again, though the shocking findings of the Independent Inquiry into Child Sexual Abuse (IICSA) on church-based sexual abuse of minors document many appalling instances of fully intentional systematic abuse, where *spiritual abuse* is concerned it is less clear that leaders *always* intentionally and knowingly target people.

Notwithstanding, these last observations are intended neither to exculpate unwitting spiritual abusers nor to diminish responsibility for harm done. As stated previously, abuse is *abuse* and it must always be challenged and addressed, regardless of the intentions or perceived intentions of the abuser. Indeed, it is noteworthy that therapists observe how the effects on victims can be equally damaging irrespective of the spiritual abuser's intentions.[28] While it is right, then, to caution that in certain cases the wolf analogy might need some nuancing – if indeed it is to be referenced at all – it remains gravely concerning that so much damage can be done by people who may be largely blind to that fact, believing, ironically, that they are doing good. How, then, might this happen, and – more to the point – how might it be prevented from happening in the spaces in which we exercise leadership? These are questions to which we will turn in Chapters 2 and 3.

Quick recap

Spiritual abuse is an abuse of power wherein a Christian leader seeks to control both the structure of an organization and the people within it. Typically, spiritual abuse manifests in behaviours that are coercively controlling, domineering, bullying and manipulative. Spiritually abusive leaders often take the moral high ground and will often misuse Scripture so as to defend their authority, screen their abusive behaviour and guilt-trip congregants into doing their bidding. Again, in order to coerce people to fall in line, spiritually abusive leaders can appeal to a divine 'anointing' and/or vocation, and regularly misuse the name of God when censuring and reprimanding those they deem to be 'disobedient' or 'backsliding'.

French psychologist and pastor Jacques Poujol identifies three types of spiritually abusive leader operating within Christian circles: the overprotective leader, the egocentric [leader] and the perverse narcissistic leader. The perverse narcissistic leader is an individual who has a dangerous psychopathic personality and perpetrates abuse – spiritual and/or other forms – in systematic, calculating and intentionally devious ways. By contrast, overprotective leaders and egocentric leaders may be somewhat unaware of their spiritually abusive behaviour and may cause damage to others collaterally and even unintentionally, but this finding is neither to exculpate them nor to play down the danger they represent. Abuse is abuse and independently of intentionality, every form of abuse must be called out.

Questions for reflection

1 What should our response be and to whom should we turn if we believe that a particular church leader or leadership group is seemingly acting in spiritually (or other) abusive ways? If appropriate, what might be the best way to *call out* leaders who are displaying signs or traits of unhealthy leadership?

2 Research suggests that some instances of spiritual abuse are committed more or less unwittingly by church leaders who believe they are doing their best for God and the people over whom they have oversight. How far should *intentionality* come into things when addressing (a) victims of spiritual abuse and (b) leaders who carry out spiritual abuse?

3 How practically can we ensure that we ourselves are safe leaders who embody a healthy leadership practice? What does leadership that is spiritually empowering and in step with Jesus' example and teaching look like?

Notes

1 Stirling, M. and Meynell, M., eds, 2023, *Not So with You: Power and Leadership for the Church*, Eugene, OR: Wipf and Stock.

2 Nick Mackison in Stirling and Meynell, *Not So with You*, p. 49.

3 See, for example, Stirling and Meynell, *Not So with You*; Honeysett, M., 2022, *Powerful Leaders? When Church Leadership Goes Wrong and How to Prevent It*, London: InterVarsity Press; DeGroat, C., 2020, *When Narcissism Comes to Church: Healing Your Community From Emotional and Spiritual Abuse*, Downers Grove, IL: InterVarsity Press; Oakley, L. and Humphreys, J., 2019, *Escaping the Maze of Spiritual Abuse: Creating Healthy Christian Cultures*, London: SPCK; Poujol, J., 2015, *Abus Spirituels*, Paris: Empreinte.

4 Stirling, in Stirling and Meynell, *Not So with You*, p. xiii.

5 Stirling and Meynell, *Not So with You*, p. 13.

6 See further Honeysett, *Powerful Leaders?*, pp. 75–9.

7 This quotation is regularly ascribed to St Augustine and it certainly coheres with ideas contained within *Confessions*.

8 This view of the church emerges, for example, in the Augsburg Confession, see the discussion in Kärkkäinen, V-M., 2002, *An Introduction to Ecclesiology*, Downers Grove, IL: InterVarsity Press, pp. 41–2.

9 Cf. on the possibility of Christian leaders lapsing somewhat unknowingly into the type of manipulative, heavy-handed and coercive behaviour patterns that characterize spiritual abuse, see, for example, Blue, K., 1993, *Healing Spiritual Abuse*, Downers Grove, IL: InterVarsity Press, p. 12; and more recently, The Anglican Consultative Council, 2019, *The Anglican Communion Safe Church Commission (ACSCC): Guidelines to enhance the safety of all persons – especially children, young people and vulnerable adults – within the provinces of the Anglican Communion*, London, p. 15. (The 'Guidelines' document is available through the Anglican Communion website: www.anglicancommunion.org.) See further, Oakley and Humphreys, *Escaping the Maze of Spiritual Abuse*, pp. 104–5; Stirling and Meynell, *Not So with You*, p. 56.

10 For early appearances of this terminology see, for example, Johnson, D. and VanVonderen, J., 1991, *The Subtle Power of Spiritual Abuse*, Minneapolis, MN: Bethany House, and particularly their justification of the terminology, pp. 22–3; Blue, *Healing Spiritual Abuse*; Oakley and Humphreys, *Escaping the Maze of Spiritual Abuse*, particularly their explanation of the terminology in relation to other forms of abuse, pp. 27–31. A minority of writers express reservations about the nomenclature 'spiritual abuse' on the premise that it might become a 'catch-all' term conflating a range of issues and potentially being misused to indict the innocent, see, for example, Honeysett, *Powerful Leaders?*, pp. 157–9.

11 Janssens, M-L., and Corre, M., 2017, *Le Silence de la Vierge:*

Abus spirituels, dérives sectaires: une ancienne religieus temoigne, Paris: Bayard, p. 15; Demasure, K., 2022, 'The loss of the self – spiritual abuse of adults in the context of the Catholic church', *Religions*, 13(509), p. 3.

12 Oakley and Humphreys, *Escaping the Maze of Spiritual Abuse*, p. 31. In a lecture held at St Mellitus College, London on 9 April 2024, Humphreys mentioned that this definition has been increasingly incorporated into the safeguarding apparatus of the Church of England.

13 Fernandez, S., 2022, 'Victims are not guilty! Spiritual abuse and ecclesiastical responsibility', *Religions*, 14(427), pp. 3–4; Oakley and Humphreys, *Escaping the Maze of Spiritual Abuse*, p. 58.

14 This is language used by Mark Stibbe in his 'Foreword' in Oakley and Humphreys, *Escaping the Maze of Spiritual Abuse*.

15 Stirling and Meynell, *Not So with You*, p. 16. Stirling's phrase is 'we cannot and must not do Jesus' work in non-Jesus ways'.

16 Poujol, *Abus Spirituels*.

17 Poujol, *Abus Spirituels*, pp. 13–24.

18 Poujol, *Abus Spirituels*, p. 15.

19 See further Johnson and VanVonderen, *The Subtle Power of Spiritual Abuse*, pp. 183–91.

20 Cf. Collicutt, J., 2015, *The Psychology of Christian Character Formation*, London: SCM, pp. 66–7 on attachment/separation issues in infancy being carried into adult life; McIntosh, G. L. and Rima, D., 1997, *Overcoming the Dark Side of Leadership: The Paradox of Personal Dysfunction*, Grand Rapids, MI: Baker, pp. 161–9.

21 Poujol, *Abus Spirituels*, pp. 15–16.

22 Poujol, *Abus Spirituels*, p. 17.

23 Poujol, *Abus Spirituels*, p. 17.

24 Cf. Stirling and Meynell, *Not So with You*; Honeysett, *Powerful Leaders?*; DeGroat, *When Narcissism Comes to Church*; Oakley and Humphreys, *Escaping the Maze of Spiritual Abuse*; Poujol, *Abus Spirituels*.

25 Poujol, *Abus Spirituels*, p. 18 '… nous ne sommes plus dans le registre des *personnes* difficiles mais dans celui des *personnalites* difficiles'.

26 Poujol, *Abus Spirituels*, p. 23.

27 Oakley and Humphreys, *Escaping the Maze of Spiritual Abuse*, pp. 113–14.

28 Oakley and Humphreys, *Escaping the Maze of Spiritual Abuse*, pp. 104–5.

2

Neither deference nor indifference

It is no good pretending that as Christian leaders we have little or no power. We do. Power and power differentials are givens in leadership. Being realistic about this is essential if we are to grasp how we affect others. We need to be as insightful as possible if we want to ensure that we use our power and authority in right and godly ways. (Marcus Honeysett)[1]

The Guidelines [Guidelines for the Professional Conduct of the Clergy] warn against bullying and the misuse of power, which can work in many different directions – clergy on clergy, laity on clergy, clergy on laity, laity on laity … There is the need for each of us to be watchful and to be ready to intervene in appropriate ways where we suspect such action for it is 'all our business'. (Robert Innes)[2]

How do church people relate to their leaders? How do we as Christian leaders *expect* that people will relate to us? What sort of power dynamics operate within our churches and Christian organizations? More pointedly, as Christian leaders, to what extent are we aware of the power we hold and the power differentials that might be at play in our interactions with those for whom we are responsible before God? Such searching questions arise inevitably in the aftermath of leadership scandals of the type referenced in Chapter 1 wherein an unhealthy relationality degenerates into patterns of co-dependency. In situations where power dynamics go askew and personal boundaries are transgressed, it should be sooner rather than later that questions are going to be asked …

So far we have reflected on the variable nature of unsafe Christian leadership, noting that in some, albeit unusual, cases abusive individuals with psychopathic traits may be intentionally predatory, presenting a significant red-flag risk to the community. More commonly, research suggests that overprotective and egocentric leaders may be somewhat unaware of their manipulative, coercive and spiritually abusive behaviours. Irrespective of motivation, the damage and trauma that unsafe leaders cause are significant. Since the behaviour of abusive leaders of any type is likely to trigger red flags, how is it, then, that such individuals are able to gain a foothold in our church communities in the first place, and what are the conditions that allow unsafe leaders to flourish?

It is my contention that the genesis and evolution of unsafe leaders may be linked to two opposite dangers, which, in the final analysis, lead to the same lack of transparency and accountability and sense that one is above suspicion (and perhaps the law) that are so dangerous. Unsafe leaders emerge and flourish where there is an unhealthy *culture of deference* but it can also be true that unsafe leaders emerge and flourish where there is an unhealthy *culture of indifference*.[3] In what follows we shall consider and attempt to describe these in turn, working towards identifying some defining characteristics of each, if not a tight definition per se.

While acknowledging that abusive Christian leaders do not necessarily need to be *ordained* leaders, special attention will be given to the meaning and nature of ordained ministry since unhealthy cultures of deference have a particular tendency to grow up around those who don the dog collar. As we explore these themes it is important to understand that such deference cultures – cultures in which ministers are regarded as 'untouchable' – can be birthed and nurtured as much by church members as by abusive church leaders themselves. The same can sometimes be true of what I am calling unhealthy cultures of indifference, where any sense of formality and structural accountability is downplayed and considered unnecessary or 'over the top'. In a word, the types of unhealthy culture that allow the flourishing of unsafe leaders tend to be marked by a level of *reciprocity* or co-dependency between leaders and church members.

Overdoing the deference

Our society has become accustomed, sadly, to stories of charlatans who worm their way into positions of power within respected institutions so as to perpetrate bullying, abusive and even criminal behaviour from a place of cover. All too often these abusers enjoy certain protections on account of their position and status within a given organization. In churches and Christian entities this can happen as – to take one prominent example – the shocking findings of IICSA (The Independent Inquiry into Child Sexual Abuse) have demonstrated so emphatically. Other scandals in the Christian world point to a misuse and abuse of power not necessarily connected to abuse that is sexual in character. What these various and variegated abuse stories tend to have in common is a skewed power dynamic resulting from an exaggerated and insalubrious culture of deference.

Unhealthy deference cultures take root when Christian leaders are put on a pedestal and treated as more important or more holy than other people. We are not talking about *respect* here – self-respect and showing respect towards others is self-evidently positive and necessary – but vertiginous deferential cultures go way beyond respect. In these cultures, the minister emerges as *the* truly knowledgeable, *the* most intelligent, *the* super-prayerful and *the* saintly-spiritual anointed servant of God to be revered before and above all others. Where the word of the pastor is so closely identified with the Word of God it is easy to see how the usual checks and balances of accountability can rocket right out of the window. On the reciprocity principle mentioned above, the unsafe Christian leader will likely own the undue deference shown to them and milk it for all it is worth. For the leader who buys into a deference culture, the adulation of their public shapes self-understanding in a distortive idolatrous and self-magnifying sense. Rather than championing the interests and wellbeing of others, the individual becomes ever more insular, self-absorbed, self-important and self-referential within their ecclesial echo chamber.

To begin with a disclaimer, and to spell out something mentioned above, you don't have to be ordained to become the focal point of an unhealthy deference culture. In recent years high-profile non-ordained church leaders have made the news, bringing themselves and the organizations they represent into disrepute. These are individuals found to be perpetrators of various forms of abuse around whom a culture of deference grew up and whose illicit activities went largely unchallenged – until it was too late. Without naming names, we are alluding to abusive activity and even shocking crimes, but crimes committed by prominent lay leaders, not ordained ministers. Of course, capable people who hold significant roles are necessary to run and maintain churches and church organizations, and we are blessed that very many highly competent individuals choose to serve in church roles. Nevertheless, there are exceptions to the rule and in unduly deferential cultures, authority figures are taken at their word and remain accountable only to themselves. The ostensibly charming *but in reality* bullying and manipulative Christian leader is liable to lean on position and status to camouflage inappropriate and harmful behaviours. Thus, before we explore the types of deference culture that can and do grow up around ordained ministers, we acknowledge that lay leaders in churches and various office holders can be regarded as in some way 'untouchable' and may take advantage of others in much the same way as can happen with clergy.

But on to ordained ministers. You don't have to venture far to find unhealthy deference cultures in which 'the clergy' are regarded as a sort of separate species and viewed as living-breathing paragons of virtue. If 'Father' appears slightly radiant, well that will be the halo! A spiritual DNA test of these serene beings would reveal abnormal levels of holiness mixed with off the charts niceness.[4] Again, *respect* is one thing, but an eye-wateringly potent dosage of deference – the type that elevates Christian leaders to the right hand of the Lord on high – extends well beyond a healthy respect. The term 'clericalism' is frequently used to describe this lofty and uber-exaggerated sense of deference that is applied to members of the clergy specifically. To paraphrase a discussion from a previous volume:

Clericalism fosters an unhealthy, unbiblical, unchristian pow-er imbalance ... [it] encourages individuals to see themselves as categorically different from and superior to others, [it] diminishes a sense of accountability [and] undermines the primary calling of the whole people of God.[5]

Dovetailing with this description, in a work principally con-cerned with addressing the dangers of clericalism, Simon Cuff defines the latter as 'a form of improper inhabiting of power [which] enables the flourishing and capacity to act of a particu-lar part of the body of Christ at the expense of the flourishing of the entirety of the body of Christ'.[6] It is clear that where clergy are regarded by others as a sort of super-spiritual elite – and come to regard themselves as untouchable – an 'improper inhabiting of power' is in itself an abuse of power and can open the door to various forms of de facto acts of abuse that impact negatively on others.

In Anglican circles 'clericalism' is routinely associated with the more catholic wing of the church, but this is unfair insofar as it is oversimplistic and does not tell the whole story. Recent scandals in evangelical churches – both Anglican and non-Anglican – suggest that an elevated and exaggerated deference culture can be symptomatic of toxic and unsafe church envi-ronments, irrespective of church tradition. To put it another way, a minister does not need to splash holy water or swing incense to be thought of as deeply spiritual and above all sus-picion. 'Clericalism' might be associated with dressing up in ornate liturgical garb but it can be present equally where the minister with magnetic charisma deliberately *dresses down*. Thus, whether a deference culture couples with magniloquent titles plus ritualistic pomp and ceremony, or whether it grows up around an evangelical modern-day prophet figure decked out in casual clothes and eye-catching trainers, clericalism of one form or another gives rise to unsafe cultures in every corner of the church.

Cultures become *unsafe* when those entrusted with leadership are believed to be above all suspicion and are allowed to rule the roost free from accountability and scrutiny. In such enclave environments clergy are seldom held accountable and rarely challenged when signs of abusive behaviour first come to the surface. Instead, where an ordained minister is well known and celebrated, people tend to turn a blind eye or seek to explain away behaviour that would ordinarily raise a red flag: 'it's just his way', or 'she is rather eccentric, you know!' Sadly, when telltale signs and warnings go unheeded, abusers will find their niche. It is then that patterns of abusive behaviour that are in no way normative can somehow become 'the norm', bringing devastating consequences for those trapped within the enclave.

In the kind of situation just described, victims are generally too afraid to disclose abuse because of the unequal power dynamic.[7] 'Why would anyone take my word *over his?*' is the common sentiment of people subjected to church-based abuse. Again, this is because of the active deference cultures that have been the scourge of Christian organizations. In churches where things have gone wrong there often seems to be something in the ether that suggests that clergy are somehow different from everyone else, that things do not apply to clergy in quite the same way that they apply to others. Since the potentially dangerous sense of entitlement and 'otherness' that attaches to clergy is both widespread and deep-rooted, we need to dig into and interrogate this perception of the underlying distinctiveness and *otherness* of ordained ministry.[8]

But aren't clergy different from everyone else?

Spanish author José Ortega y Gasset once asked: '*¿De qué materias extrañas está hecho el hombre inglés?*' – 'From what strange materials is the Englishman made?', which is probably a fair question (but perhaps one that an Englishman ought not attempt to answer!)[9] To riff off Ortega y Gasset we might enquire, '*Of what strange materials is the ordained minister made?*' What kind of being is this strangely attired person who these days attracts trust and suspicion in almost equal measure? Who is that person who grows accustomed to answering to bizarre appellations such as 'curate, vicar, Father, Mother, pastor, Reverend' and stands out from the crowd on account of their somewhat archaic dress code?

More pointedly, what effect does the imposition of hands and the invocation of the Holy Spirit at the moment of ordination have on a person? Is there a sense in which at some fundamental level of their being the one who is ordained undergoes a sort of mystical and spiritual transformation? Are we right to conceive of something along the lines of that which Anglo-Catholic clergy term *ontological change*? And if we accept the idea that there is some sort of transformation that occurs deep within us at the point of ordination, what does that change entail, how might it be expressed and what does it mean for our life and ministry after ordination?

Within Roman Catholicism there has long been the sense that those who enter the priesthood *should be* regarded as a special class of persons. This notion is indexed, arguably, to beliefs about apostolic succession and works on the premise that priestly ordination effects a profound and mystical transformation in the ordinand. Thus, at the First Vatican Council it was openly and explicitly stated that the status of the clergy is *different* from that of the laity, and that the Church is a 'society of unequals' within which it is the prerogative of the clergy (and not the laity) 'to sanctify, to teach and to govern'.[10] True, various statements arising from Vatican II sought to soften and row back from the rather stark rhetoric of the earlier Council. Nonetheless, it is clear that an innate clericalism persists in certain segments of Roman Catholicism. A few years ago a Roman Catholic archbishop could state, 'As priests, we can't go back and become "merely human" again, because we are not.'[11]

Within Anglicanism and other churches I suspect that the vast majority of ordained ministers would balk at the notion that on account of our ordination we are no longer 'merely human'! As Bishop Graham Tomlin puts it:

> Clergy are human beings. That, hopefully, can be taken for granted (although some understandings of priesthood make them so distinct from humanity that they become almost like a separate race of people altogether, like the old Irish joke

where there were three sets of public conveniences: one for Men, one for Women and a third for Priests).[12]

Quite so. As we have been suggesting throughout this chapter, unhealthy cultures of deference abound where an overegged understanding of ordained ministry confers on mere human beings a sort of demi-god status. Alarmingly, where clergy are regarded (and regard themselves) as a 'separate race of people altogether' there is likely to emerge a tacit acceptance that in their case the normal rules simply do not apply. Therefore, a culture of clericalism and exaggerated deference provides the perfect incubator for the growth of unsafe spaces where unsafe leaders can flourish to the detriment of all who find themselves in their 'care'.

Again the reciprocity element rears its ugly head. Whatever clergypersons may think of themselves and the nature of their Orders, it is clear that some very unhelpful projections are brought to bear on ordained ministers. Floating around in our churchy ether are a plethora of preconceived ideas that speak to what the minister ought to be and do – reinforcing stereotypes that tend to undergird the faulty understanding that clergy are fundamentally and *categorically* different from everyone else. In this vein John Williams hits the nail on the head when he draws attention to the 'theological "otherness"' that attaches to members of the clergy:

> The theological 'otherness' of priesthood readily turns into a whole set of projections of apartness on to priests by society at large: morally, in that priests must be holier than the rest of us, woe betide them if they fail; spiritually, in that priests will have perfect prayer lives and always be untroubled by doubts; culturally, in that priests mustn't drink (too much) or smoke or know anything about sex; or socially, in that priests live in some other world and aren't part of 'ordinary life'.[13]

While church members and society at large are perhaps unlikely to state baldly that clergy exist as a kind of 'separate race', the unrealistic and unfair expectations that are often projected onto clergy do rather encourage unhealthy levels of deference and standardize special treatment. In other words, the ways in which people think of and relate to ordained ministers suggest that the latter are treated *as if they were* ethereal creatures gliding about the place in a special existential category all of their own! Again, where idealistic projections colour and cloud the picture of who ordained ministers really are – and what we should and should not expect from them – bad and abusive leadership can go under the radar or, worse still, it can be detected but remain unreported.

To be clear, while I wish to debunk the notion that ordained ministers make up some kind of elite class of superhuman or quasi-angelic being enjoying an exclusive hotline to the Most High, I am denying neither the importance of ordination, nor the fact that ordination changes things. Baldly, ordination *does* change things and things change at ordination. If you were to ask around I think you would find that most clergy would agree that something changes – or some things change – at ordination. Certainly, things are never the same following that spiritually charged moment. Inwardly, there may be a sense of the transforming effect of God's grace and the weight of responsibility that ordination confers, though this is not to be confused with the misconception that the ordained person becomes somehow free from sin or more holy than others through the rite of ordination (cf. the Thirty-Nine Articles of Religion #26). Outwardly, in the swearing of ordination oaths there should be a sense of the change that occurs in terms of the role and responsibility that one is taking on as a public minister in the Church of Christ. Again, the latter should not be understood to mean that in their new role and life clergy need no longer be accountable – just the opposite in fact.[14]

Given the dangers of clericalism with its temptation to regard 'the clergy' as a spiritual elite, it is important, therefore, that we provide a clear answer to the question about *how* things are different following ordination. If it is true in some way that ordination effects a form of change in those who enter Holy Orders, it is equally true that much remains the same. As an ordained person I am no holier, no more worthy and no better than I was before I was ordained just because I have been ordained. True, I will be made *more accountable* and be held to high standards by the church and ultimately by Christ himself in virtue of my ordination vows, but that does not give me any right to demand special treatment or to think of myself as being above the systems and processes that we are all rightly subject to in church and society in general. On the contrary, at the risk of stating the obvious, clergy ought to lead by example. Therefore, in matters such as safeguarding and practices related to 'safe church', for example, clergy must be 100 per cent pro-active in ensuring that they are first in line so as to be fully up to speed in the relevant areas and swift to acknowledge that they are as accountable if not more accountable than everyone else.[15]

Dialling down the indifference

If an overdose of deference sits at one end of the spectrum, at the other extreme are ill-judged and frankly embarrassing attempts to downplay any sense of the 'otherness' of ordained ministry. In some circles ordained ministers seem to be at pains to appear 'just like everybody else' and 'completely normal' (whatever on earth that means), but in a way that is painfully forced and weirdly counter-intuitive for clergy. I don't consider myself to be prudish but I admit to being slightly taken aback when in a first meeting with one Church of England priest (now quite senior) her very first sentence was an expletive-laden tirade about something or other. This pales into insignificance alongside a male vicar from back in the day, who, legend has it, was referred to by parishioners as the 'effing vicar' because of his rather liberal and ill-tempered use of the 'F-bomb', often within the confines of the sanctuary itself!

Habitual bad language is one thing but, more broadly, something is not quite right when clergy insist on playing down or even denying altogether the distinctive character of the life and work of ordained ministry. Without getting carried away into clericalism, most Christians would acknowledge that there is a genuine 'otherness' to ordained ministry, which needs to be acknowledged, respected and upheld. We are talking about a deeply meaningful calling that finds its vocation in nurturing and serving other vocations within the body of Christ. We are talking about a role that carries significant responsibilities in regard to the care of others, where – in the case of Anglican ministry – oaths are sworn and promises made as people sign up to be answerable and accountable to their bishop under God. But this can all seem at odds with the type of self-image that some ministers project through online platforms and with how they present in person.

The social media profile of the pastor that screams 'I'm too cool for school' is par for the course within a flamboyant culture of informality. Again, this isn't so much a dig at a particular form of dress code or the lack of one, merely the observation that certain hipster church cultures can sometimes become rather self-contained and unhelpfully subversive. Existing in a sort of bubble, in various Churches of the Anglican Communion I have witnessed how low-church guru-type leaders eschew ministerial titles and codes, cultivating a sort of passive–aggressive indifference towards those to whom they are actually accountable in ecclesiastical law. Thus, within Anglicanism one meets these smooth-talking mavericks who are typically aloof or downright non-compliant when it comes to overseers. Whatever we think of the people tasked with steering the ship – and bishops are as human and fallible as everyone else (let's get it right!) – such disdain towards authority is deeply concerning because accountability structures are put in place for a reason.

As stories of spiritual and other types of abuse have sadly revealed, trouble can be just around the corner where church workers sit lightly to formal church structures. Unsafe leaders wreak havoc by taking a relaxed *laissez-faire* or a grudgingly feet-dragging approach towards ecclesiastical process and protocols such as those in the area of safeguarding. Indifference towards overseers and accountability systems not only means that unwitting spiritual abuse can go unchecked, but it sends out all the *right* signals to those who harbour predatory intentions and seek an environment in which to plot *wrong* things. In the somewhat rare but hardly unprecedented cases where ministers themselves harbour abusive intentions, informality can combine with *faux* humility (or 'fauxnerability' to reference DeGroat's term, Chapter 3) and a deceptive semblance of openness where people are drawn into relationships that are not appropriately boundaried. A lone-wolf minister may turn out to be exactly that ...

Sometimes it can be difficult to find the right balance and an indifference towards external authority can be an understandable reaction against heavily clericalized structures. For sure, where deference culture is a problem there is a bit of an issue with the optics of prostrating before the bishop in an ordination service or kissing the episcopal ring. I am aware of at least one senior leader within the Church of England establishment who now refuses to use the 'bishop' title when speaking to bishops. On a visit to St Mellitus College a student asked them, 'What if the bishop insists that you address them with the "bishop" title?' To which they replied, 'I would insist that it is better that I use their first name only!' While I appreciate the bold rationale of anti-clericalism behind this sentiment, for me personally, this probably goes too far.

The Brazilians have a great little expression, *nem oito nem oitenta* – literally, this translates as 'neither eight nor eighty', meaning that it is best to avoid extremes and to procure a more balanced and moderate approach. Such an approach acknowledges that generally speaking it would be wrong to throw out the bishop with the bathwater! What is needed to restore the equilibrium is a proper understanding of the role and responsibilities of clergy (from deacons to bishops) and a right appreciation of the 'otherness' of ordained ministry, understood in vocational terms. If we want to pursue a leadership model that produces safe Christ-like leaders, then neither a heavily deferential culture nor a culture of indifference will do. Instead, a more balanced approach must encourage a thoroughgoing mutuality aiming at healthy levels of mutual respect, mutual accountability and mutual care.

Quick recap

Closely linked to cases of spiritual and other forms of church-based abuse are overdeferential cultures that encourage 'clericalism'. Clericalism elevates church workers, principally ordained leaders, to an exaggeratedly high position, wherein ministers are regarded (and may regard themselves) as morally and spiritually superior to others. Within deference cultures accountability structures can be lacking or downplayed because the 'anointed' leader is thought to operate on a higher plane, rendering such accountability unnecessary or even insulting. In a parallel way, cultures of indifference can similarly eschew accountability mechanisms wherein church workers sit aloof to formal church structures. Though the minister may dress down, on the surface of things wearing their clerical status lightly, indifference and/or resistance to central structures and overseers such as bishops can lead to the propagation of unsafe environments.

Neither a culture of deference nor a culture of indifference is desirable if we are to foster safe church contexts stewarded by safe church leaders. Healthy organizations are characterized by cultures of mutual respect and mutual accountability, where structures and overseers are seen as fundamental to a flourishing and happy environment. This is as true of the church and para-church organizations as it is of any other institution or entity.

Questions for reflection

1 Why is it that cultures of deference make churches unsafe or potentially unsafe, and is it the case that clericalism is only a thing in more 'catholic' or traditional-leaning churches?

2 In your own leadership or future leadership role, what practical steps might you take in order to prevent clericalism from getting a grip on you and your ministry?

3 What are the characteristics of a culture of indifference and what can church leaders do to ensure that they are transparent and properly accountable to overseers?

Notes

1 Honeysett, M., 2022, *Powerful Leaders? When Church Leadership Goes Wrong and How to Prevent It*, London: InterVarsity Press, p. 21.

2 Harrison, J. and Innes, R., eds, 2016, *Clergy in a Complex Age: Responses to the Guidelines for the Professional Conduct of the Clergy*, London: SPCK, p. 114.

3 The link between 'clericalism' (i.e. an exaggerated deference culture in reference to church leaders) and abuse is made in the important work of The Anglican Consultative Council, 2019, *The Anglican Communion Safe Church Commission (ACSCC): Guidelines*, p. 27.

4 Biological tests would presumably indicate a predominance of caffeine and strong traces of overwork, but we won't go there for now ...

5 Throup, M., 2022, *When Jesus Calls*, Norwich: Canterbury Press, p. xiv.

6 Cuff, S., 2022, *Priesthood for all Believers: Clericalism and How to Avoid It*, London: SCM, p. 9.

7 For more on these themes, see (ACSCC): *Guidelines*, pp. 8, 20.

8 The 'otherness' of ordained (priestly) ministry is an idea explored by Williams, J., 2020, *Ecclesianarchy*, London: SCM, p. 67.

9 Ortega y Gasset, J., 1988, *Notas de Andar y Ver: Viajes, Gentes e Paises*, Madrid: Alianza Editorial, p. 218.

10 In Dulles, A., 2002, *Models of the Church*, New York: Image, p. 30.

11 A citation of Archbishop of Glasgow Philip Tartaglia speaking in 2017, in Williams, *Ecclesianarchy*, p. 66. The broader context of the quotation (as registered by Williams) is a rebuttal of the notion that priests should think of themselves as being 'just like everyone else' and Archbishop Tartaglia's point is well made. Nevertheless, the framing of language in this description of priesthood leans heavily into a clerical paradigm.

12 Tomlin, G., 2014, *The Widening Circle*, London: SPCK, p. 114.

13 Williams, *Ecclesianarchy*, p. 67.

14 See Harrison and Innes, *Clergy in a Complex Age*, and the Professional Guidelines for the Conduct of the Clergy helpfully reproduced within that publication.

15 In this vein within the Anglican context it is encouraging to read the 'calls' of the bishops of the Anglican Communion in the Lambeth Call Safe Church document under point 4 – published in May 2023 'as part of the third phase of the Lambeth Conference journey' – where, for example, the bishops commit to 'ensuring we ourselves are equipped with the necessary knowledge, understanding, compassion and discernment through training, listening to the experiences of those who have experienced abuse and ongoing sharing with fellow bishops'. The

document is available for download at www.anglicancommunion.org, the website of the Anglican Communion. Alongside a range of people including representatives from the Anglican Communion Safe Church Commission I was invited to contribute to a training event organized by CAPA (Council of Anglican Provinces of Africa) for African bishops and their spouses that took place in Maputo, Mozambique in the summer of 2023, which in the African context began that 'equipping' process mentioned in the Lambeth Call document.

3

Showmen with the gift of the gab

[The issue] is an ever-increasing dependence upon individuals, focusing on magnetic personalities and great gifting rather than on Christian character, such that certain leaders effectively become untouchable. We have placed them on such a pedestal that they can effectively do what they like. (Steve Wookey)[1]

Underneath the carefully manicured exterior, the real story is of a man who seemed, according to many, to have a megalomaniac desire to control other people ... (Roland Howard)[2]

Praise God for those extraordinarily gifted and genuinely godly ministers engaged in wide-reaching gospel ministry that is a great blessing to a great many people! Every so often we might hear about or even meet such truly *extraordinary* leaders (cf. Chapter 5) whose servant-hearted commitment to Christ and whose bold pioneering spirit bear much fruit through years of dedicated service. Such leaders are marked out by remarkable giftings, but giftings rooted in authentic discipleship and the tenacious pursuit of a Christ-like character. For exactly this reason they themselves procure no pedestal, and though their names may be well known it is the name of Jesus they seek to make known. Our *extraordinary* leaders are those who have risen to prominence but for whom fame and fanfare are more a burden than a blessing.

So let me be clear here: the critique sketched out in this chapter is not to be applied willy-nilly. It is in no way aimed at the Spirit-led and truly inspirational individuals who exercise healthy leadership and in so doing are such a blessing and encouragement to our communal life. Those wonderful and genuinely Christ-like leaders are a far cry from that sorry cadre of self-centred *showmen* who cultivate private personality cults. Thus, the spotlight in this chapter falls squarely on *showmen* leaders who cynically misuse the pulpit as a podium for self-promotion. The object of the *prophetic heckling* in the pages that follow is to expose the questionable leadership style of figureheads who talk a good game but whose actions contradict their words. It is these performers whose ministries can prove so damaging to others and so detrimental to the gospel.

Over several decades in the UK and overseas church scenes we have seen how time and again high-profile leaders on stratospheric trajectories can fail and rapidly nosedive. The scandals come in all shapes and sizes and are diversely nuanced. Sometimes the personal failings of a pastor can lead to a tragic error or series of errors that damages others and simultaneously derails the ministry of that pastor. Sometimes the ego of the ecclesiastical star or wannabe celebrity is so hyperinflated that the sheen of their own reflection blinds them to the destructive effects their power-crazy and spiritually abusive behaviour has on others. Chillingly sinister are the cases of church workers who make ministry about themselves by design, whose misdeeds are calculated, premeditated and systematic. 'Who knew?' becomes the sorry interrogative in the dreadful aftermath of church leadership gone wrong, but people brushing abusive behaviour under the church carpet is a story that has become all too familiar. Sometimes the congregation are in denial and where winsome *showmen* weave their magic the wool can be pulled over their eyes.

Where ministries have borne fruit over years, effecting a largely positive shaping influence on a place or even a generation, it can be especially difficult to square the circle when a prominent leader is exposed as an untrustworthy person. Alas, every branch of the Christian faith has its share of sickening abuse stories authored by charlatan leaders living a double life. To reiterate something said earlier, it is not my intention to discuss the detail of any specific case that has come to light in recent years – sadly, we are not short on examples and the list of names only lengthens. Rather, I want to draw attention to a leader *type* and a leadership *style* that I believe to be fundamentally at odds with the gospel of Jesus Christ. The leader type that to all intents and purposes seems truly incompatible with a true ministerial vocation I am calling the *showman* leader. The style of leadership that is wholly incompatible with Christian ministry I am terming the *spectacular.*

By *spectacular* leadership I mean that which seeks to become a spectacle for its own sake – self-obsessed leadership that loves the big stage and looks to make a big splash for its own self-glorification. *Spectacular* leadership is typified by the pumped-up personality driven by selfish ambition – the all-singing all-dancing *showman* who insists on making lots of noise but for selfish reasons. Big-time ministers who embrace *spectacular* leadership can be de facto celebrity leaders and household names or they can be the proverbial big fish of the local pond. To describe these leaders I am going with the gendered term *showmen.* This seems appropriate because – let's be honest here – most leadership scandals implicating high-profile Christian leaders or wannabe celebrities centre on men. That said, some high-flying women ministers embody a grandstanding *spectacular* leadership that manifests in spiritually abusive behaviour, so we will use 'showmen' as a convenient catch-all term to cover both men and women for whom ministry is or ultimately becomes a megalomaniacal crusade.

Spectacular leadership and *showmen* leaders

What I am calling out as *spectacular* leadership tessellates with the profile of the egocentric leader explored at the beginning of Chapter 1. At its worst, such leadership – if for argument's sake we may call it leadership – prioritizes self-aggrandizement, the unsavoury flip side of which is a propensity to diminish and discredit others. *Spectacular* leadership in church circles is all about self-projection. It glories in the show, the sparkle, the razzmatazz of the hyped-up entrance centring on the guru with the gift of the gab and the pulsating demagogy of sermonic stucco. Unhappily, I have encountered this celebrity-culture

Christianity on four continents. Underneath the shiny veneer of polished performance one will sometimes encounter a modern-day Simon, the misguided sorcerer of whom the people had mistakenly claimed: '"This man is the power of God that is called Great"' (Acts 8.10). So desperate was he for attention, recognition and status that Simon sought to purchase the power of the Spirit (Acts 8.18–19). In much the same way *showmen* leaders crave attention, recognition and status to such an extent that they will do everything in their power to achieve *greatness*, using a distorted version of religion, ritual and spirituality as the means to pursue that end.

Though not always the case, *spectacular* leadership can some-times combine with the warped agenda of *prosperity theology* – the 'faith industry'. Here a minister's rather conspicuous objectives concern the selfish pursuit of societal status and the accumulation of personal wealth where money is extorted from the congregation in a form of spiritual blackmail. On one occa-sion in Florida, I sat and squirmed as an immaculately dressed pastor bellowed at his congregation, irate that someone would dare to question his authority as the 'anointed prophet of God'. For 40 minutes I listened uncomfortably to a 'sermon' that, in reality, was an extended tirade and a thinly disguised attempt to justify the luxurious lifestyle of the prosperity preacher. Years later at an airport in Rio de Janeiro I winced as a well-known televangelist and prosperity pastor signed autographs for fans under the watchful eye of his personal security guards! As the flight was called, said televangelist shoved and elbowed his way past people in a dash for the front of the queue, *the first shall be last* ...

Among the survivor voices contained in Chapter 1 was the example of an anonymous small-time UK church in the 1980s whose wannabe *big-time* leaders scolded and sidelined those suffering from long-term illness on account of their supposed 'spiritual disobedience' and 'faithlessness'. This side of the pond there are fewer examples of full-blown prosperity theology, though dubious 'imports' and imitations can be found in our cities. Nonetheless, where *showmen* strut their stuff one will sometimes find the appalling tropes of a wrong-headed health–wealth cult. More commonly, subtler forms of the health-and-wealth movement can crop up in home-grown Pentecostal and charismatic evangelical circles. A kind of *light-touch* prosperity gospel can copy and paste elements of this fake theology without going all in on the shameless quest to accrue personal wealth through the ministry. Again, many leaders in general and *showmen* leaders in particular are wont to measure ministerial 'success' in mainly numerical and – at times – material ways. Frequently, pastors can be heard taking credit for construction projects, showing pride in plush settings or magnificent buildings. Of course, there is nothing wrong with nice buildings, but the minister who talks up their ministry on the grounds of materiality may be missing the point – or even papering over the cracks of spiritual deficit.

Whether motivated by power, status, money, the thirst for *success* or a combination of these worldly things, *showmen* leaders are invested in keeping up appearances. Like the pharisees roundly criticized by Jesus in Matthew 23, they always seek the best seats in the merry-go-round of church engagements and local events. *Spectacular* leadership craves power and gravitates towards the powerful. Woe to you, *showmen* leaders, who sidle up to dignitaries and VIPs with exaggerated gestures and sycophantic small talk! You dabble in the dialect of name-dropping and in the company of the influential seek puppy-eyed for a sign of recognition! Woe to you, champions of *spectacular* leadership – hypocrites! For you the people who matter most are *those who have* – money, prowess, pedigree, the right sort of schooling, influence, connections. Woe to you and your self-congratulatory churchy elitism! Woe to your classist respectability, which moves quickly to make acceptance of persons, but spurns the little children and prevents them from coming to Jesus!

Of course, *showmen* leaders talk the talk of *servant leadership* but they will not walk the walk. Subtly or unsubtly, *spectacular* leadership comprises a perverse parody of the leadership of the Lord Jesus inasmuch as it is self-seeking and comes to be served and not to serve. As a result it is committed to an implacable pursuit of personal projects and the unremitting non-compromising promotion of self. It is secretly – or not so secretly – displeased with the success of others, which it regards as an outrage, a personal insult and an open threat. Those who pursue *spectacular* leadership tolerate no rivals and take no prisoners. Many years ago when I was in parish ministry in South America I discovered that one such *showman* leader viewed me as a rival and a threat to his popularity, which, by the way, I really wasn't! Before long I found that I was being uninvited to church events in which I had been slated as the keynote speaker. Talk about cancel culture! In my place, inevitably, would appear the name of the celebrity leader who had changed the plan without deigning either to notify me or to explain why.

Whether it is obvious or stealthily kept under wraps, *spectacular* leadership is relentlessly committed to the furtherance of *my* ministry, *my* church, *my career* (where 'career' is the operative word). As per the adage, there is no 'I' in the word 'team' and the *showman* leader has no thought for collaboration, though they will inevitably surround themselves with 'yes' men and *Martha* women. This is a pseudo version of 'ministry' that *does to* rather than *serves with*, incarnating a spellbinding theatrical performance that aims to garner plaudits and groom followers. On the one hand it craves more and more attention, but *spectacular* leadership refuses to be accountable, instead monitoring and marshalling its tightly guarded inner circle in a one-way forced accountability – a studied and sustained attempt to maintain control. Here the congregation is treated rather like the mirror, mirror on the wall of the fairy tale, comprising an *audience* expected to offer up adulation and applause so as to affirm and nourish the ego of the self-acclaimed 'power-posturing' super-leader.[3]

The *spectacular* prioritizes the profile and prizes 'optics'. *Showmen* leaders procure influence by adopting a pushy salesperson demeanour. Social media offers up the perfect platform to pontificate and pose online. On any given medium the totemic leader waxes lyrical to a self-congratulatory beat, indulging in scripted and clichéd inanities – 'Fantastic that ...', 'Wonderful to be at ...', 'Grateful to ...' – when all the while the subtext and crypto-messaging transmit the tediously monotonic, monosyllabic algorithm of the first person singular. Are the *showmen* even remotely aware of their unchecked egotism and burgeoning narcissism?

But to be clear, *showmen* leaders do have a knack for drawing people in. We are talking about charismatic personalities who know how to work a room, spin a yarn and woo a crowd. We call this *spectacular* leadership for a reason. The *showmen* are capable of putting on a spectacle, though whenever they take centre stage they do so with the conviction that they themselves are the main event. Think larger-than-life figures who exude a kind of quasi-mystical magnetism, oozing irresistible charm and panache. Think magicians who possess a seemingly innate ability to wow onlookers with their repertoire of tricks. Again, these may be imposters who *play the game*, entertaining notions of grandeur packaged in lofty ambitions, but we are talking about genuinely gifted people nonetheless. And 'gifted' may be understood in straightforward human terms, but also in terms of spiritual gifts. An associate of a church leader who was asked to step down from ministry on account of several allegations of inappropriate behaviour 30-odd years ago reflected the following: 'I now see him as a man with a tremendous spiritual insight and psychic power, who made good use of his abilities for his own ends and resisted allowing the searchlight to rest on him.'[4]

Gifted *showmen* leaders can indeed make good use of their abilities to service their own agendas and this plays out in a range of attitudes, actions and behavioural traits. In *When Narcissism Comes to Church*, Chuck DeGroat runs through a catalogue of behaviours that can manifest in those who default to a narcissistic *spectacular* leadership style. While these include what we may identify as 'standard' traits, for example, centralizing all decision-making and intimidating others to gain and retain control, more subtle tendencies are also traced, for example, 'praising and withdrawing' and what DeGroat terms 'fauxnerability'.[5] While the former is fairly self-explanatory, relating to the power dynamics of control in the relationship between the leader and those in their in-crowd, the latter is a 'twisted form of vulnerability' referring to how the *showman* leader may sometimes present.[6] Whereas in much *spectacular* leadership there is the outward projection of the 'strong man' leader image, on occasion false vulnerability may be shown. Thus, crocodile tears or oversharing from the pulpit may be used to elicit sympathy or a 'support vote' from the congregation. Ultimately, such 'fauxnerability' amounts to a strategy to protect one's position and/or deflect blame or responsibility. Marcus Honeysett picks up and explains this further:

> Fauxnerability is an emotionally intelligent strategy whereby a carefully calculated display of weakness and emotional messiness is designed to influence people to respect and like us, creating dependency. It is a form of carefully concealed narcissism and relational domination disguised as openness and meekness ... fauxnerability provides a way for leaders to be applauded by churches for *appearing* weak without actually having *to be* weak ... Fauxnerable leaders may realize they are doing it, or it may have become so ingrained as to have become their natural, subconscious way of working.[7]

Appalling church scandals testify to the guile with which notoriously narcissistic leaders can deploy a range of strategies creating a sort of pseudo-spiritual subterfuge to camouflage abusive activities indexed to their predatory perversions. But to recall Poujol from Chapter 1 and to revisit Honeysett's final sentence above, whether abusive leaders are *perverse narcissists* who intentionally prey on church members or whether because of some underlying psychological deficiency they are *egocentric* figureheads potentially unaware of the deleterious effects of their behaviour on others, abuse is abuse. Irrespective of intention abuse is abuse and unsafe leadership leads to people getting seriously hurt. Tragically, when the whistle is blown doubt can be cast on the courageous testimony of abuse victims because the *showman* leader enjoys the status of a saint and holds the power of office. In many cases abusive leaders are shielded from accusations by the loud protestations of their card-carrying entourage. Perhaps as human beings there are times when the truth can be staring us in the face, sitting right under our nose, but it can be so dreadfully unpalatable that we simply refuse to believe it.

Unquestionably, in the post-IICSA era it ought to be beyond question that no-one is beyond question. And yet, so often the people taken in and mesmerized by the charm and charisma of shaman-like *showmen* are complicit in their silence or in their remonstrations when the awful and seemingly unacceptable truth comes to light. Just as we observed in regard to cultures of deference and indifference (see Chapter 2), so in specific relation to *showmen* leaders the principle of reciprocity or co-dependency obtains. *Spectacular* leadership makes its home where church members seek a strong leader to idolize. *Showmen* nurturing personal projects feed off people who seek support, being drawn in only to be left out in the cold. And just as a convincing lie contains a grain of truth, unscrupulous *showmen* exploit the fact that deep down we all crave community, we all long to belong.

Ultimately the current crises in Christian leadership can be located within broader trends arising in the contemporary Christian scene. Here the biting comments of Brazilian theologian Ricardo Barbosa are food for thought:

> There is a crisis in contemporary Christian spirituality. What we see out there are pastors, church members and church workers who are avid for models of church growth, self-help or the latest fashions in worship. These are formulas that seek to respond to the new demands of modern times, but when we look at the churches, leaders and church members in general, we do not see the presence of Christ. What we see are Christians who are enthusiastic about *worship*, leaders who are committed to showcasing their own projects and ministries, churches that transform themselves into a kind of 'religious brand name', giving a certain 'status' to those who frequent them ...[8]

If we are to right the wrongs of recent decades then we must confront *spectacular* leadership and challenge *showmen* leaders whose commitment is first and foremost to 'showcasing their own projects and ministries' and whose first love is themselves. It is a twisted *theology of glory* that morphs ministry into performance and knows nothing of the cruciform trajectory of genuine discipleship. Enough of *spectacular* leadership and the self-indulgent celebrity culture that builds the 'religious brand name' at the expense of the Kingdom! Enough of firework leaders who rocket skywards with promise but fizzle out and crash down with chaotic and traumatic fallout! What we need right now is a whole other way of approaching Christian ministry and leadership. For what it is worth, I think we need perfectly *ordinary* leaders who are committed to a prosaic and pedestrian *unspectacular* leadership.

Quick recap

Spectacular leadership that manifests in unabated self-promotion, grandiose personal projects and careerist empire-building involves a clear misuse and misappropriation of Christian ministry. Delve below the surface of church-based abuse scandals and very often you will uncover egocentric leaders bewitched by narcissism who have embraced the *spectacular*. Some are charlatans who position themselves at the centre of purpose-built ecclesial ecosystems whose activities constitute an intentional abuse of power. Others may be deeply self-absorbed and less aware of their selfish and damaging egotistical behaviours that so traumatize others. *Showmen* leaders come in all shapes and sizes, from celebrity leaders with global renown to big characters who rule the roost in a local bubble. Whether they are well known or mere wannabes, selfish ambition and a disproportionate need for recognition, affirmation and acceptance are what ultimately drives such leaders and often leads to situations of spiritual abuse.

Questions for reflection

1 What differentiates gifted Christian leaders whose life and ministry are a blessing from *showmen* who embrace a form of *spectacular* leadership?

2 What is meant by the term 'fauxnerability'?

3 In your own leadership or future leadership roles, how can you avoid the pitfalls of *spectacular* leadership?

Notes

1 Wookey, S., in Stirling, M. and Meynell, M., eds, 2023, *Not So With You: Power and Leadership for the Church*, Eugene, OR: Wipf and Stock, p. 119.

2 Howard, R., 1996, *The Rise and Fall of the Nine O'Clock Service*, London: Mowbray, p. 5.

3 '"Power-posturing" simply means that leaders spend a lot of time focused on their own authority and reminding others of it, as well. This is necessary because their spiritual authority isn't real – based on genuine godly character – it is postured'. Johnson, D. and VanVonderen, J., 1991, *The Subtle Power of Spiritual Abuse*, Minneapolis, MN: Bethany House, p. 63.

4 Howard, *The Rise and Fall of the Nine O'Clock Service*, p. 24.

5 DeGroat, C., 2020, *When Narcissism Comes to Church: Healing Your Community from Emotional and Spiritual Abuse*, Downers Grove, IL: InterVarsity Press, p. 70.

6 DeGroat, *When Narcissism Comes to Church*, p. 82. In the ensuing sentence I draw once more on this helpful section, cf. pp. 83–4.

7 Honeysett, M., 2022, *Powerful Leaders? When Church Leadership Goes Wrong and How to Prevent It*, London: InterVarsity Press, pp. 55–6.

8 Barbosa, R., 2012, *Identidade Perdida*, Curitiba: Encontro, p. 126, my translation and emphasis (in italics).

PART 2

An alternative leadership paradigm

4

Towards *unspectacular* leadership

Not to us, O Lord, not to us, but to your name give glory,
for the sake of your steadfast love and your faithfulness.
(Psalm 115.1)

Either your life is about Jesus and his mission or it is about
you. There is no third option. (Robert Barron)[1]

Unspectacular leadership is the antidote to spiritually abusive leadership. It is the antithesis of the noxious clericalism and shameless *showmanship* called out in previous chapters. *Unspectacular* leadership is unglamorous leadership. It seeks no drumroll to announce its presence and procures no limelight in which to bask. It is content to be a footnote in the Kingdom purposes of Christ and is in no hurry to make any headlines of its own.[2] Instinctively self-giving rather than self-seeking, *unspectacular* leadership strives to be responsive to the needs, joys, pains and struggles of the community. In traditional Church of England speak this is leadership that prioritizes the 'cure of souls', and strives to show the compassion of Christ to everyone in a given locality. To paraphrase some famous first-century poetry, *unspectacular* leadership is marked out as being 'patient, kind, not envious or boastful or arrogant or rude, neither insisting on its own way nor resentful, rejoicing in the truth' (cf. 1 Corinthians 13.4–6).

Unspectacular leadership is 'patient' in that it sticks with and by people, refusing to give up on them notwithstanding the let-downs and the heartache that can be part and parcel of the pastoral task. It is 'kind' since it operates within the sphere of grace and mercy, being shaped by the divine kindness on which it leans and relies. Because it is Christ-centred and not self-centred and because it is Christ-focused and not self-fo-cused, it is neither 'envious or boastful or arrogant or rude'. Unlike spiritually abusive leadership it does not insist on getting its own way. Unlike the *showmen* who resent the talents, suc-cesses and popularity of others, *unspectacular* leadership is not 'resentful'. Unlike the toxic culture of clericalism, which sustains the Orwellian lie that 'all are equal but some are more equal than others', the *unspectacular* 'rejoices in the truth' that 'all are one in Christ Jesus' (cf. Galatians 3.28). *Unspectacular* leader-ship is the leadership of love in action; it is spiritually healthy leadership and leadership that releases people into life in Christ.

Unspectacular leadership rejects a self-oriented, self-refer-ential, self-promoting 'my way or the highway' approach to interaction and asks with genuine interest 'how are *you*?' On this model the question is not 'how can I …?' but 'how can *we* …?' Without negating their impact or underplaying the poten-tial of their ministry, practitioners of *unspectacular* leadership are circumspect when it comes to their own importance and quick to emphasize the value of others. To paraphrase the saintly Mozambican Bishop Dinis Sengulane, a Christian leader who played a crucial role in brokering peace in his country after 16 years of civil war: 'I am "important", but in the sense that I am made in the image and likeness of God, loved by him – that makes me important!'[3] Those who quietly practise *unspectacular* leadership within our churches and parachurch organizations are the unsung heroes who, keeping one eye on heaven, are disarmingly down to earth.

Unspectacular leadership, then, is characterized by Christ-shaped humility. Uninterested in status, unconcerned with 'career', unimpressed by social standing and untainted by titles, such leadership, one might hypothesize, is more Galilean than urbane, disinclined to overegg its own importance but always talking others up metaphorically. In its efforts to circumnavi-gate the sinking sands of secular consumerism, *unspectacular* leadership journeys unapologetically within a biblical world-view, resting, ultimately, on the rock that is Christ. Those who choose to step into this unpretentious pattern of leadership can travel with confidence, assured of the divine hope and grace that sustain. *Unspectacular* leadership is self-aware but not self-consumed. Practically, it is receptive to feedback and practised in the art of weighing and sifting words that may be weaponized against it (cf. 1 Thessalonians 5.20). Again, it offers scripturally rooted counsel but encourages the hearer to weigh any word that is given, being cautious to differentiate its own voice from the voice of God.

As Graham Tomlin points out in *The Widening Circle*, the apostles and early Christian theologians are not referred to in the New Testament as 'leaders' in the typical Greco-Roman vocabulary (Greek *archon*), for such authoritarian figures were the secular *showmen* of their time.[4] Our New Testament authors have studiously avoided this language because these arrogant *archons* were the guys who indulged in first-century *spectacular* leadership with its politics of 'bread and circus', interested merely in feeding their own popularity to further their personal agendas. This is hardly the pattern of leadership we see in the example of Jesus. Thus, in contrast, those biblical passages that speak of Christian leaders use words such as 'overseers' and 'deacons'. That which is required of them is deeply significant, albeit somewhat *unspectacular* on the surface of things.

The shape of *unspectacular* leadership

The apostle Paul sets out some expectations for church ministers in 1 Timothy 3, explaining that among other things they are to be 'temperate', 'sensible', 'respectable', 'hospitable', 'apt to teach' and 'gentle'. Again in the letter to Titus, 'overseers' are to be 'blameless', neither 'arrogant nor quick-tempered', not 'addicted to wine or violent or greedy for gain', but 'hospitable', 'lovers of goodness', 'prudent', 'upright', 'devout' and 'self-controlled'. Those exercising senior leadership in churches are to have 'a firm grasp of the word' in order to 'preach with sound doctrine and refute those who contradict it' (Titus 1.7–9). Nothing here then about an ability to woo a crowd with spellbinding speech, nothing on winning over the masses with grandiose gestures or extravagant displays of miraculous healing. The priorities of *unspectacular* leadership lie elsewhere, namely in the development of a Christ-like character and the ordinary exercise of day-to-day prayerfulness. This form of leadership prioritizes the pursuit of godliness and the patient work of discipling the body of Christ in accordance with 'sound doctrine'. This is pastorally adept, authentically Christ-shaped leadership, leadership that espouses a rounded, gracious and right use of Scripture rather than a heavy-handed misuse of certain 'go-to' scriptures.

Several of the New Testament epistles warn about counter-feit ministers and imposters, stressing the need for authenticity on the part of Christian leaders. For instance, in Titus 1.16 there is a warning about those 'who profess to know God, but ... deny him by their actions', and the well-known verses in James about double standards seem to set up his sober counsel, 'Not many of you should become teachers, my brothers and sisters ...' (James 3.1, cf. 1.22–27). Back in the seventeenth century in a classic work on pastoral ministry Richard Baxter warned against hypocrisy, emphasizing the need to 'study our own hearts'. For Baxter, 'if it be not your daily business to study your own hearts, and to subdue corruption, and to walk with God – if you make not this a work to which you con-stantly attend, all will go wrong'.[5] And the remedy to prevent everything from going wrong? 'Above all, be much in secret prayer and meditation,' advises Baxter.[6]

Rather more recently, the Church of England has put together a framework for the formation of ordained ministers revolving around several 'Qualities' that Christian leaders are expected to inhabit and display. These include 'Love for God', 'Love for People', 'Wisdom', and 'Trustworthiness'. In their own way the Qualities and the detailed expectations written into them are a template for what I am calling *unspectacular* leadership. Thus, following ordination when a fledgling minister is serving their curacy (Church of England speak for something like a junior pastor post), they are expected to be 'growing in Christlike character in daily living for example in love, humility, patience, prayerfulness and obedience'. Again, there is the expectation that the leader 'has empathy and is aware of how others receive them' as well as the requirement to be 'a mature and integrated person of stability and integrity'. Not only must they demonstrate 'good listening skills', but they have to 'accept fair criticism with maturity' and 'acknowledge and live with their own vulnerabilities'.[7]

It is clear from the language of the Qualities that the Church of England is working hard in its processes of discernment and ministerial formation in order to guard against charlatans and *showmen* type leaders. As well as giving consistent and studied attention to safeguarding, there is a special emphasis on the growth and development of a Christ-like character. Here the attributes that are required of ministers stand in marked contrast to the shenanigans of *spectacular* leadership and the destructive behaviours of spiritually abusive leaders. Thus, there is the requirement of curates to 'reflect critically on their own and others' use of authority and power, understanding the dynamics operating within the local church and responding with wisdom and humility'. Once more, new ministers are expected to 'understand(s) their own conscious and unconscious bias (having) strategies to mitigate them', and to be able to 'face the challenges of ministry including its disappointments with equanimity'.[8]

Further to this focus on the development of a healthy Christian character, the determination of the Church of England to stop spiritually abusive behaviour at source is inherent in the quality of 'Trustworthiness'. Admittedly, in leadership and in life 'trust' and 'trustworthiness' form 'a nebulous concept'.[9] It is difficult to assess the extent to which a person is or is not worthy of our trust. No-one wants to be deceived and fall prey to a scammer or someone intent on taking advantage. On the other hand it is easy to be judgmental and to be swayed by personal biases, whether or not we are aware of these. Objectively, what the Qualities for ministerial formation are looking for in the apprentice minister are consistent behavioural patterns and demonstrable characteristics that align with a form of leadership that is genuinely Christ-shaped and can therefore be trusted. Overall, in their day-to-day ministry, curates are expected to exhibit a 'high degree of self-awareness' and to 'lead maturely' following Christ 'in every part of their life'.[10]

This latter consideration around being an *integral* disciple of Christ is of particular relevance to what we have been exploring in relation to spiritually abusive leaders and *spectacular* leadership. In their early study on spiritual abuse Johnson and VanVonderen pondered what they termed the 'double life of false spiritual leaders', where the words of the Christian worker are disconnected from the reality of his or her actions in real life.[11] Now in the case of charlatans such dissonance, double standards and hypocrisy are largely a conscious thing, part and parcel of their cynical modus vivendi. On the other hand some leaders may slip into unhealthy behaviours and addictions either consciously or subconsciously. Here there is a sort of compartmentalization of life so that the front of house looks rather different from what is going on backstage.[12] These leaders may well detest the moral mess that is not on show, trying to suppress it through pure willpower and compensatory attempts at holiness. However, Johnson and VanVonderen caution against attempts to 'subdue [the sinful behaviour] with firm resolve' while neglecting 'to deal with and heal ... the wounds and motivations that lie beneath the surface of the external behaviors'.[13]

Unspectacular leadership aims to 'lead maturely', and it works on the premise that the individual leader is committed to following Christ 'in every part of their life'. There can be no compartmentalization. There can be no dichotomization. As the Puritan Richard Baxter cautions all church ministers, 'Take heed of yourselves ... lest you unsay with your lives, what you say with your tongues.'[14] More poignantly still, it is worth digesting what Roman Catholic theologian Robert Barron states so baldly: 'Either your life is about Jesus and his mission or it is about you. There is no third option.'[15] Similarly, theologian-martyr Dietrich Bonhoeffer famously said, 'When Christ calls a man, he bids him come and die ...', adding, 'The call to discipleship, the baptism in the name of Jesus Christ means both death and life.'[16] If we are to live integral lives in Christ we must confront the stuff that needs confronting and take the daily decision to die fully to self.

To put it another way, in order to be trustworthy in leadership we have to *get real*. If we recognize in ourselves a latent tendency to compartmentalize or to suppress sinful behaviour without dealing properly with the 'wounds and motivations that lie beneath the surface' then we need to get help. Meaningful self-reflection will involve being honest with ourselves and others before things really go south. We will have more to say on getting to grips with our inner life without beating ourselves up or doing ourselves down when we come to discuss self-care (see Chapter 7). For now we note the advice of Oakley and Humphreys who urge us to 'dig deep to maintain a focus on ourselves' and to 'invest time in our own development as leaders for the sake of those we lead'.[17]

Whereas *showmen* and spiritual abusers can hide behind the mask of a fraudulent and fake piety, showing no interest in changing, authentic leadership not only acknowledges its humanness and vulnerabilities but confronts these with honesty, seeking healing and a *metanoia* new direction. Positive steps are made when leaders seek out the help of mentors, counsellors and professionals. Authentic leadership is trustworthy leadership and to expand this a little further, it is leadership marked out by the threefold hallmarks of 'credibility', 'reliability' and 'relationality'.[18] *Credible* leadership is leadership that knows what it is talking about and not only talks the talk but walks the walk! *Reliable* leadership is constant and consistent leadership, leadership that delivers on its promises. *Relational* leadership is leadership that is personable and relational in character, leadership that is transparent with the other person about its agenda, unwaveringly committed to mutuality.

Advocates of this credible, reliable, relational *unspectacular* approach to leadership are disinclined to throw themselves forward, but remain ready to step in as and when called upon. When others are losing their heads this is the type of leadership that steps up without fuss in the heat of a crisis. It is trustworthy leadership on account of its uncompromising transparency and its consistently open, honest and undefended approach. What you see is what you get, and no amount of faff or fanfare could ever trump such straight-laced authenticity. While those who embrace this leadership may have godly and goodly ambitions, they forgo the illusions of grandeur that so typify those who buy into the *spectacular*. Possibly with the helping hand of time and experience, practitioners of *unspectacular* leadership have divested themselves of delusional careerist thinking, or more probably they undergo periodic internal examination, working hard to keep a lid on pride with the support of trusted mentors. Such leaders tend to be open, down to earth, unashamedly real and thoroughly realistic about themselves and others. They are realistic about both the opportunities and the limitations presented by their own humanity and that of those in their care.

Midfield generals and metronomes

My 11-year-old son has just become captain of the local football team and is playing in midfield. He is working on what it means to (a) play in midfield, and (b) captain the side. (For those unfamiliar with football and/or unfond of extended sports analogies, please bear with me!) Playing in midfield involves *hard work*, *situational awareness* and *tempo*. By *hard work* I mean lots of running. It is about running when your team has the ball, for instance passing and moving, linking play, creating/supporting attacks, and bursting forwards with the ball. If that sounds exhausting, it is equally if not more taxing when your team loses or does not have possession of the ball since midfielders have to sprint to close down space, to mark opposition players and to get in a tackle so as to stifle an attack. Within football it is common knowledge that Premier League midfielders run over 10 kilometres in every game they play!

It is not all about the physical side, though. Midfielders have to know how and where to position themselves so that they can become the glue that binds together the defence and the attack. This requires good *situational awareness* and an intelligent 'reading' of the game. Now you cannot always be in the right place at the right time but a good midfielder 'reads' the game so that they are in the right sort of zone, always on hand to help out a teammate, see off a threat or find the space to surge forwards. Perhaps the most difficult skill to attain in football is this ability to see the bigger picture and to react to each scenario accordingly. A lack of situational awareness results in a ton of huffing and puffing and players careering about the pitch like headless chickens – not good!

Finally, midfielders are the key to how a team plays insofar as they set the *tempo*. A good midfielder can control the rhythm of a game, speeding up interconnecting passes in order to build an effective attack, or slowing down the game to give players a breather and ensure everyone is in the correct position. This is where the idea of a 'metronome' comes in, something used in music to keep the beat and to help musicians stay in time as they play. The 'tick', 'tick', 'tick' of a metronome provides the steady pulse that underlies and sustains the music.

By now you have probably guessed how this sporting cum musical analogy can be applied to our thoughts on Christian leadership. Those who embrace *unspectacular* leadership are comparable to midfielders in that they are *hard-working*, have *situational awareness* and help set the *tempo*. Hard work is a fact of ministry. Too often hard work can become overwork – something we must guard against – but ministry will always mean running hard (which is why, of course, self-care and scheduled rest/retreat periods are essential to ministerial life, cf. Chapter 7). Like a lot of defensive midfield play, much of this hard work goes unnoticed and is unglamorous but it is absolutely essential. Ensuring the paperwork gets done is hardly the pinnacle of excitement but in a church or parachurch context competent administration keeps everything on track. Again, being a stickler for safeguarding training and checking that staff are up to speed and that buildings are in good repair all require effort, but these things are vital so as to keep people safe and help the team manage risk.

Similarly, *situational awareness* is paramount for people tasked with leading churches and Christian organizations. In ministry this is often about understanding group dynamics and 'reading' people. It is about seeing the bigger picture but also the detail of a given situation and being ready to react in appropriate and sensitive ways. Such awareness and action require self-confidence but the sort of quiet understated confidence of *unspectacular* leadership rather than the extravagant overconfidence and bluster of the *showmen*. An awareness of what is going on in the moment and what is coming down the line is a basic characteristic of leadership. Sometimes this will require taking a step back and seeing how a set of interactions play out. On other occasions it will be necessary to step in and do some sorting out. Here the order of the day are people skills and a willingness to be on hand to help out, offer a steer or guard against potential dangers.

Unspectacular leadership is also about team players who can be instrumental in setting the *tempo*. Just as a midfielder can act a bit like a metronome, keeping the ball moving and the team ticking over, so a committed church leader seeks to be a consistent and constant presence for the good. Again, the midfield metronome might not be the player with flair making all the headlines, but without their dedicated service the team just won't perform. Indeed, if the person responsible for setting the *tempo* turns out to be a showboating *showman* more interested in exhibiting their flashy ball skills than bringing others into play then the team becomes too dependent on that centralizing figure and neither grows nor flourishes.

Many of the traits described above are also integral to what it means to captain a football team or indeed any sort of team. For example, hard work, availability, a disposition to serve others and the ability to keep the team ticking over. In sport you will hear commentators and pundits say that someone put in 'a captain's performance', by which they mean the captain led by example and – when necessary – pulled the team up by its bootstraps! A 'captain's performance' will be characterized by a 'can-do' attitude but also by service and a selflessness that puts the team above the personal interests of any individual. Tapping into our discussion above, it is clear that a good captain not only talks the talk but walks the walk. Any captain who simply shouts at others demanding that they do this, that or the other without lifting a finger themselves is not a true leader. Any captain who seeks individual glory over the flourishing of the team has not understood what true leadership is all about. In Christian ministry, true leadership patterned on the example of Jesus will always seek to edify others, and it will consistently look like *unspectacular* leadership.

Quick recap

In Christian circles *unspectacular* leadership tends to stay out of the limelight and the headlines, quietly going about God's business with dedication and determination. This type of leadership displays the characteristics that are required of New Testament 'deacons' and 'overseers' and is marked out by its uncompromising commitment to developing a character that is Christ-shaped and Christ-focused. In contrast to the *spectacular* leadership of *showmen* leaders, *unspectacular* leadership is credible, reliable and relational. Whereas fake and narcissistic leaders fail to address and confront their blind spots, *unspectacular* leadership takes personal vulnerabilities seriously, adopting an 'undefended' approach. Typically, practitioners of *unspectacular* leadership are hard-working, show situational awareness and set the tempo within a team.

Questions for reflection

1 What words would you use to describe *unspectacular* leadership?

2 What does a 'credible', 'reliable' and 'relational' form of ministry look like in practice? Can you think of Christian leaders you know who embody and model this sort of approach?

3 Some people are called to take a lead role in a church organization and to be that 'go-to' person and it is inevitable that power attaches to certain church leadership roles. How, according to the *unspectacular* leadership paradigm, might church leaders use their position and power healthily, and what can they do to ensure that their leadership remains healthy?

Notes

1 Barron, R., 2021, *The Strangest Way: Walking the Christian Path*, Parkridge, IL: Word on Fire, p. 139.

2 I am reminded of a comment made by N. T. Wright about wanting to be a footnote in God's Kingdom purposes, though given the voluminous nature of Wright's writing I am unable to recall where exactly this note appears.

3 Bishop Dinis Sengulane, in an address to a group of African bishops, their spouses and visitors from various Provinces of the Anglican Communion as part of a training event for new bishops held in Maputo, Mozambique, 27 July 2023.

4 Tomlin, G., 2014, *The Widening Circle*, London: SPCK, pp. 135–6, cf. pp. 139–40.

5 Baxter, R., 1979, *The Reformed Pastor*, Edinburgh: The Banner of Truth Trust, p. 62.

6 Baxter, *The Reformed Pastor*, p. 62.

7 From the Qualities for Ordained Ministry IME 2 (curacy) grid, which grid can be accessed via the Church of England website: www.ime-2-priest-pioneer-qualities-and-evidence-from-autumn-2022.pdf (churchofengland.org).

8 Ibid.

9 Poole, E., 2017, *Leadersmithing: Revealing the Trade Secrets of Leadership*, New York: Bloomsbury, p. 155.

10 See the Qualities for Ordained Ministry IME 2 (curacy) grid at note 7 above.

11 Johnson, D. and VanVonderen, J., 1991, *The Subtle Power of Spiritual Abuse*, Minneapolis, MN: Bethany House, pp.122–3.

12 For a more in-depth treatment of a similar 'front' and 'back stage' idea, see Walker, S. P., 2010, *The Undefended Leader*, Carlisle: Piquant, pp. 2738.

13 Johnson and VanVonderen, *The Subtle Power of Spiritual Abuse*, p. 123.

14 Baxter, *The Reformed Pastor*, p. 63.

15 Barron, *The Strangest Way*.

16 Bonhoeffer, D., 1996, *The Cost of Discipleship*, London: SCM, p. 79.

17 Oakley, L. and Humphreys, J., 2019, *Escaping the Maze of Spiritual Abuse: Creating Healthy Christian Cultures*, London: SPCK, pp. 125 – 6.

18 This threefold schema (and the couple of sentences in my text) are adopted and adapted from Poole, Eve, 2017, *Leadersmithing: Revealing the Trade Secrets of Leadership*, London: Bloomsbury Business, p. 155, which in turn draws on the 'Trust Equation' of David Maister, Charles Green and Robert Galford where trust is a function of a person's *credibility, reliability and intimacy*. 'Relationality' here just seems to me to be a more straightforward and less misunderstood term than 'intimacy', thus the switch in my own formulation.

5

Reclaiming the ordinary

Aspire to live quietly, to mind your own affairs, and to work with your hands ... (1 Thessalonians 4.11)

So I commend enjoyment, for there is nothing better for people under the sun than to eat, and drink, and enjoy themselves, for this will go with them in their toil through the days of life that God gives them under the sun. (Ecclesiastes 8.15)

Maybe it is just my imagination but I suspect that Koheleth, the preacher and author of Ecclesiastes, and I would get on rather well. I reckon he would approve of bank holidays. He would certainly approve of my activities so far this sun-kissed bank holiday weekend. These include:

1 Catching up with friends over a beer (a zero one in my case, but that's for health reasons so I reckon he would give me a pass).
2 Watching football from the vantage point of my sofa.
3 Doing a spot of barbecuing on the terrace.
4 Painting the garden fence with a special wood-protecting formula.
5 Making the car look vaguely respectable with a smidgeon of wax and a bucket load of elbow grease.

Depending on your age and stage in life you might be looking at that rather blokey five-point list thinking it completely sad, or you might be smiling to yourself knowingly. For a middle-aged man like myself – proud owner of the proverbial pipe and an actual pair of slippers – this is what dreams are made of! To be honest, these days it does not take much to make me happy.

With the aid of time and experience I have realized, albeit belatedly, that ambition is overrated. 'Success' is entirely relative, and as for the pursuit of wealth (chance would be a fine thing) that is a mere exercise in 'chasing after the wind'. For those of us blessed enough to have the privilege of a peaceful existence, experience teaches that it is much better to stick to the simple things in life. You might say that Koheleth captured the essence of it when he opined, 'Go, eat your bread with enjoyment and drink your wine with a merry heart ...' (Ecclesiastes 9.7).

Scholars debate the extent to which Koheleth should be identified with Solomon, the wise king of Israel. Either way Ecclesiastes seems to have been written by a wise, if at times incorrigibly negative, person. In the manner of all self-respecting middle-aged men, as per the quotes above, Koheleth prizes common sense and a good old-fashioned slap-up meal. Why wouldn't you? He sure as *sheol* won't stand for any *showman-like* shenanigans and, at the risk of projecting my own prejudices onto him, I suspect he would have struggled somewhat with social media and the excesses of our twenty-first-century culture! I can well imagine that his oft-repeated catchphrase 'there is nothing new under the sun' doubled as a verbal bodycheck for bright young things fresh out of wisdom school. A word from the broody Koheleth silences the whizz-kids, fending off their latest theories and newfangled ideas! While he is by no means the archetypal antihero, Koheleth is every bit the curmudgeon. I identify with him insofar as he loves a good grumble and – on a bad day – will insist on his glass-half-empty outlook. But underneath it all he is all right. He gets it.

In his brighter moments, what Koheleth sees so lucidly is that which we have so often lost sight of. The blessing of the *ordinary*. The daily gift of the everyday. In a world that can make little sense, a world in which our questions sometimes outrun any answers, taking the time to contemplate the ordinary can bring us back down to earth in a good way. During those times when our faith seems absurd and the fact of our very existence sets out its stall as a largely insoluble conundrum, the blessing of the ordinary serves as a reminder that there is an understated magnificence to the mundane, a sense that God-given normality is sacrosanct and that life is precious. A 'normal' conversation over coffee is gold dust, the chitter-chatter of songbirds an exquisite symphony, a walk in the countryside a stepping into the sheer goodness of the divinely crafted creation.

The contention of this chapter is that in church leadership too, there is a sense in which 'ordinary' is something to be prized and pursued, something to be *reclaimed*. We can all be wowed by star performers and idealize superhero figures – whether these be genuinely good guys or *showmen* with an agenda – but woe to us if we overlook those leaders who are quietly acquitting themselves to the glory of God! Perhaps it is natural to want to *be like* the successful leader who is a blessing and in every sense *extraordinary*, but what about the *ordinary* leader whose *unspectacular* leadership channels the grace of God in simple faithfulness and whose steady presence keeps an organization afloat? If you consider yourself to be 'run of the mill', an 'average leader', 'nothing special' then take it from me that the church needs leaders exactly like you! Above all, to paraphrase some thinking from a previous volume, we need leaders who are extraordinarily *ordinary*![1] In a word, we need leaders who are 100 per cent committed to being 100 per cent themselves!

From truly *extraordinary* to perfectly *ordinary* leaders

I was sat in the upper echelons of the Royal Albert Hall. The immaculate self-made billionaire stepped up to the stage to rapturous applause. This, this was the human embodiment of 'success', the incarnation of achievement right there before our very eyes. And fair play to him. Here was a truly *extraordinary* man. The type that does a half-marathon before arriving at the gym and who swims a few miles in the bitterly cold sea while the rest of us are fumbling around for the elusive 'snooze' button on our alarm! A person so ultra-organized that spreadsheets are a second language and time is managed down to the millisecond at the tap of a stylish-looking smartwatch. Dogged determination mixed with a strong dose of innovative intelligence and a generous sprinkling of business acumen had rocketed this remarkable individual to the very top of the tree. Truly *extraordinary* ... and fair play to him.

I was sat in the front row of a graduation ceremony in London. The Archbishop took the microphone and a hush came over the audience. This, this was a true theologian, the purveyor of a seemingly inexhaustible well of wisdom right there before our very eyes. And fair play to him. Here was a truly *extraordinary* man. As much a polymath as a polyglot, the Archbishop possesses a truly prodigious memory and the ability to deliver a talk entirely without notes, though as if he were reading from a meticulously redacted and mellifluously crafted script. 'Oh no, he never writes anything down,' his wife confirmed, as starstruck I asked how on earth he did it! Truly *extraordinary* ... and fair play to him.

From time to time we meet extraordinary and inspirational people like those described above. Shining lights in their field, it is no surprise that such exceptional figures are flown in for leadership seminars or wheeled out for graduation speeches. I want to be clear that there is nothing inherently wrong with being *extraordinary*! At university we had a guy on the sports team who would jog five miles to get to the pitch, put us to shame by running around five times more than anyone else during the game, and then sprint the five miles back to college! I knew of one aging professor of theology who was rumoured to start his day with a swim in the Cherwell before mattins and remained sharp as a razor all day while students (like me) stumbled through lectures trying to stay awake, never mind anything else. Whatever you think of her Margaret Thatcher, so they say, would only ever sleep for an hour or two – *extraordinary*. Now there may or may not be a smidgeon of exaggeration in such anecdotal accounts but the feats of such remarkable people are quite *extraordinary* all the same.

Whether it is about DNA, downright discipline or a combination of both, some people are simply wired in a way that enables them to function, well, a little differently from the rest of us. They are *extraordinary* and deserve to be acclaimed as such. I have absolutely no problem with that. What does strike me as problematic, however, is the elevation of the extraordinary to the obfuscation of the ordinary. By the 'elevation of the extraordinary' I have in mind the subliminal or the transparently blunt messaging that insists, 'If you want to succeed, you need to be like him! To fulfil your potential, you need to live your life as she does!' This sort of messaging is standard in the vast body of literature produced by self-help gurus, and unhappily you will also find it on rinse and repeat in Christian conferences, podcasts and publications on leadership or vocation. Albeit with good intentions, we seem determined to set about making a rule of that which is clearly an exception. All too often, we promote the cult of comparisons and judge ourselves and others by someone else's standards. We are all probably guilty of this in more or less conscious ways but we need to be careful.

What seems to be lacking in much of our thinking about leadership is proper perspective on self and proper perspective on life itself. The proper perspective on self supplied by a salutary theological anthropology is what I am talking about. In short, permission to be comfortable in my own skin because this is precisely the skin that God created for me and the skin he meant me to inhabit! Yes, those people over there are truly *extraordinary*, and we give thanks to God for each and every one of them and all their remarkable feats! But just as two and two don't make five, the fact that someone standing over there is genuinely *extraordinary* does not mean that there is something wrong with me for being a little *ordinary*. Far from it. At the risk of stating the theologically obvious, from a Christian perspective any and every *ordinary* person created *imago Dei* is quite extraordinary and remarkable enough as it is. 'Run of the mill' is pretty special given that you were created as a chip off the old divine block! And yet ... and yet we seem to cling on to a leadership template that pressurizes perfectly ordinary folk into striving to become something they will never (and should never) be. It is really quite extraordinary that we do this!

If you'll humour me for a second, it is absolutely OK for someone to go steaming down the Autobahn at 120 miles per hour in their shiny new race-tuned supercar – if that is what they want to do – but it is equally OK for me in my trusty 12-year-old jalopy (true story) to pootle along at 60 mph in the slow lane. While I may or may not feel a tinge of envy as they zoom past, any attempt to manoeuvre my trusty jalopy into the fast lane so as to emulate the supercar's breathtaking speed and acceleration would be wholly inadvisable. Drive a perfectly normal car to and beyond its limit and the result of such red-lining will be inevitable breakdown compounded by a long wait for recovery. Similarly in church leadership, attempts to emulate the extraordinary efforts of others and to shun the ordinary are a sure recipe for painful breakdown and a long recovery process.

In theory we know all this, don't we? Milestone publications such as John Mark Comer's *The Ruthless Elimination of Hurry*[2] and Paul Swann's *Sustaining Leadership*[3] comprise a much-needed shot across our bows or an injection of common sense into our spiritual bloodstream. Nevertheless, in our Protestant work ethic on steroids, we beaver away towards burnout, showing care for others but regularly turning a blind eye to the physical alarm bells going off left, right and centre in our own bodies. Very often our church institutions are complicit. Declining membership and dwindling funds present those in authority with agonizing and frankly impossible decisions about the allocation of resources. 'Revd Kev is looking after four churches at the moment but, er … he could probably take on a couple more, couldn't he?' 'Revd Sheila is a safe pair of hands and she is doing such a great job on the ground, I hear … Let's give her the Safeguarding portfolio and have her *volunteer* to do some teaching on Saturdays!'

Once again it is astonishing that the impact of a global pandemic – an event that gave us a once in a lifetime opportunity to reset and in theory taught us that it is OK to be human and to take a breather – has not managed to unseat a superhuman *extraordinary* paradigm of leadership. Such a paradigm is an unforgiving master who demands of us 'work harder, be sharper, run faster, cover more ground', all the while whispering, 'You owe it to God and yourself … now, get to it!' On the face of things the mantra seems to be 'You can achieve more with less –

if only you put your mind to it ... just look at these great leaders over here!' If we didn't know better we would be forgiven for thinking that our pastors and church workers are operating on the basis of a medieval works–righteousness gospel. But any theology that involves working your way to heaven by working yourself to death is doubly dangerous and should not be touched with a bargepole.

The point that by now you may think I am labouring *ad nauseam*, but which I think must be stressed *ad infinitum*, is that 'extraordinary' is not for everyone. *Extraordinary* does exactly what it says on the tin. In other words it is *extra* 'ordinary', that is, as derived from Latin, it indicates that which is outside or beyond the orbit of the ordinary. By definition *extraordinary* is about the few not the many, about the exception not the norm. It is completely OK and quite normal to admire exceptional and extraordinary leaders. It is fine to be inspired by their genius and encouraged by their example to pursue excellence in our own ministry (which, by the way, is why in Anglican spirituality we commemorate the saints). On the other hand it is not OK to compel yourself to attempt to do exactly the things they do in exactly the way that they do them. Your mission – should you choose to accept it – is to be your wonderful God-made and God-loved self! Sometimes it takes a while to land but wake up and smell the coffee: you are *you*. Remember, as a perfectly ordinary person you are 'fearfully and wonderfully made' (cf. Psalm 139) and there is much that God wants to do in and through *you*. While we are at it, I'm pretty sure that God is very keen on you being *you* and not so keen on you striving to become a cheap knock-off version of someone else.[4]

So what does *ordinary* look like?

To revisit our discussion in Chapter 4, *ordinary* leaders pursue the type of leadership that we have described as *unspectacular* leadership, being 'credible', 'reliable' and 'relational' leaders. In a word it is 'faithfulness' that form the defining characteristic and benchmark for such leaders and above all *ordinary* leaders are faithful leaders. While faithfulness to Christ may sometimes end in martyrdom, it does not necessarily equate to 'success', particularly where 'success' is defined in the myopic categories and irrepressible immediatism of our consumer culture. We must be watchful not to measure *faithfulness* to Christ merely in terms of numbers and stats, whether the figures refer to bums on seats, likes, followers, clicks, views or whatever. It is easy to slip into what has been aptly termed 'numeritis', and most leaders – not just the poster boys and girls of *spectacular* leadership – are susceptible to exaggerating for effect so as to play the numbers game.[5]

I am reminded here of a sobering story told by the Dean of St Mellitus College, Russell Winfield, who was previously a missionary in some of the remotest parts of Canada. Those who know Russell know that he loves a good old-fashioned Bible study, and during his time ministering to a distant community Russell set up a midweek Bible study, which he advertised both in Sunday services and more generally around the place. Each week he would organize the chairs, prepare the refreshments and pray patiently that folks would attend. For the months in which he was based in this wintry outpost he kept up this routine, waiting weekly for people to come, diligently spreading the word, but no-one came. No-one *ever* came.

To be honest, when I first heard this story I found it heartening! It very much resonated with some of my more disheartening mission and parish experiences in the UK and South America (if I am being honest, the ones I tend to talk about less!). It reminded me also of these self-satirizing and tragi-comic lines from Welsh poet R. S. Thomas' 'The Minister':

I held a *seiat*, but no one came.
It was the wrong time, they said, there were the lambs,
And hay to be cut and peat to carry ...
I began a Bible class;
But no one came,
Only Mali, who was not right in the head.
She had a passion for me, and dreamed of the day ...

I opened the Bible and expounded the Word
To the flies and spiders, as Francis preached to the birds.[6]

Numbingly negative experiences such as those described by R. S. Thomas help us to recognize that some things we try in ministry may never take off, no matter how much prayer and effort we pour into them. Moreover, it is natural to feel down when people pull out every excuse in the book to circumvent the very event you are ploughing your life into! While the highs are food for the soul, the lows of normal day-to-day church work can drive you round the bend and force you to question all you hold dear. But faithfulness means standing firm and sticking to the task while sticking close to Jesus, whatever the visible and quantifiable 'results' of ministry may be. When things are tough it is vital to remember that *faithfulness* to Christ can never amount to *failure* – however 'successful' or otherwise a particular venture or strategy might be or might appear to be.

Quick recap

For those who have eyes to see and ears to hear there is inherent beauty in the innumerable simple things of this God-given life. Similarly, there is something beautiful in the simplicity and straightforwardness of *ordinary* leaders who 'aspire to live quietly' and go about God's business in unpretentious and uncomplicated ways. The ordinariness of faithful prayer, diligent reflection and regular introspection at the foot of the cross is an ordinariness to be celebrated and owned. It is easy to be lured into the cult of comparisons and, while genuinely extraordinary leaders doing extraordinary things for God can be an inspiration, attempts to become somebody that we are not will inevitably end in frustration and a sense of failure. *Ordinary* leaders are faithful leaders, and faithfulness to Christ does not always equate to 'success' in the way our consumer-driven society measures 'success'.

Questions for reflection

1 Who are the *extraordinary* leaders that you greatly admire and have proved to be an inspiration in your life and ministry?

2 What are the dangers inherent in leadership seminars and resources that point us in the direction of *extraordinary* leaders?

3 In your own context and within the context of your own calling, what does it mean to be an *ordinary* leader?

Notes

1 See Throup, M., 2022, *When Jesus Calls*, Norwich: Canterbury Press, pp. 47–8.

2 John Mark Comer, 2019, *The Ruthless Elimination of Hurry: How to Stay Emotionally Healthy and Spiritually Alive in the Chaos of the Modern World*, London: Hodder & Stoughton.

3 Paul Swann, 2018, *Sustaining Leadership: You are More Important than Your Ministry*, Abingdon: The Bible Reading Fellowship.

4 I am reminded here of Rowan Williams' reflection in Williams, R., 2003, *Silence and Honeycakes: The Wisdom of the Desert*, Oxford: Lion, p. 95: 'At the Day of Judgment, as we are often reminded, the question will not be about why we failed to be someone else; I shall not be asked why I wasn't Martin Luther King or Mother Teresa, but why I wasn't Rowan Williams'.

5 Ineson, E., 2019, *Ambition: What Jesus Said About Power, Success and Counting Stuff*, London: SPCK, p. 96.

6 Thomas, R. S., 1973, 'The Minister', in *Selected Poems 1946–1968*, London: Hart-Davis, MacGibbon, p. 23.

6

Pedestrian pastoring and unsensational preaching

So many people come to church with a genuine desire to hear what we have to say, yet they are always going back home with the uncomfortable feeling that we are making it too difficult for them to come to Jesus ... Does not our preaching contain too much of our own opinions and convictions, and too little of Jesus Christ? (Dietrich Bonhoeffer)[1]

The people of God were taught the truth of bread and the word of God in the wilderness as they walked three miles an hour by the three mile an hour God. (Kosuke Koyama)[2]

On a visit to Jerusalem some years ago I tagged along with a group of South American church leaders as we weaved our way through the bustling streets of the city. Leading the small entourage was an exceptionally tall pastor who knew Jerusalem well. Not only was this man very tall but he had a stride to match. We soon found ourselves struggling just to keep up with him as he strode out ahead in a near Olympian-paced 'walk'! On occasion our reluctant guide would slip around a corner and for a few uncomfortable seconds we would lose him from sight. Much of the time as we tried desperately to keep up, our group felt that we were missing the opportunity to take in our surroundings properly. Worse still, we feared that our striding guide – who barely ever looked back – might give us the slip, and leave us hopelessly lost in the labyrinthine arteries of the city!

In a familiar metaphor, the Christian life is compared to a journey, a pilgrimage and a daily walk with Jesus Christ. This is fitting given that the early Christian movement was known simply and charmingly as 'the Way' (cf. Acts 19.23). Pastoral work is a core ingredient of church ministry and it is all about walking with others as they journey with Jesus. Pastoral *accompaniment* comprises exactly what the term suggests, that is, it is predicated on 'walking with' other Christians as they walk the path of discipleship. While fake pastors and *showmen* leaders hare ahead insisting rather irritably that others simply follow their lead and keep pace with them, the true Christian leader seeks to accompany others by meeting them where they are. To pick up our theme, *unspectacular* leadership is the leadership that has understood that God 'walks "slowly"':

> God walks 'slowly' because he is love. If he is not love he would have gone much faster. Love has its speed. It is an inner speed. It is a spiritual speed. It is a different kind of speed from the technological speed we are accustomed to. It is 'slow' yet it is lord over all other speeds since it is the speed of love.[3]

On reading this quotation from Japanese theologian Kosuke Koyama, I'm reminded of the Parable of the Good Samaritan (Luke 10.25–37). Three people encounter the stricken man who has been badly beaten by bandits. Only one, however, is willing to slow down. You will recall that the priest 'saw' the injured man but 'passed by on the other side'. In exactly the same way, the Levite 'saw' the person in need but similarly 'passed by on the other side'. We are not told why the priest and the Levite fail to slow down. We are not told why these religious leaders choose to go out of their way to avoid the person in need instead of stopping to help them as any God-fearing person should. Maybe the priest and the Levite are too afraid to stop because of the evident threat of bandits? Perhaps there is a concern about ritual purity since the victim is described as 'half-dead' and contact with a dead body would cause ceremonial defilement?[4] Or is it that these ministers are simply too busy to help out? Perhaps these churchy leaders are so 'task-focused', so concerned with 'heavenly things', that they rather instinctively sidestep the ailing man on the ground, barely noticing him?

Writing about 'things that stifle compassion' Joanna Collicutt observes that our failure to notice those in need comes from 'preoccupation', i.e. those moments when we get bound up in our own complex thought processes.[5] Collicutt adds that irrespective of whether we are concerned with 'worthy' or 'base' things, to become unduly wrapped up in our own thought world is to risk missing what is going on around us.[6] For sure, in ministry our pastoral peripheral vision becomes impaired when our minds are struggling to keep up with all the stuff that needs doing. Therefore, to exercise effective pastoral care and to embody a pastoral presence it is essential to slow down and become attentive to what is going on both within us and around us.

Now it can take real effort to steady our rhythms so as to find that 'inner speed' or 'spiritual speed' that Koyama identifies with the 'speed of love'. We are used to moving at a million miles an hour as we flick from one screen to the next, from one message to another – we are unused to slowing down. Thankfully there are ready-made resources that can help us. Thus, in the Anglican way of being the day-to-day rhythms of Daily Prayer help put the brakes on our twenty-first-century tendency to rush right into things in blinkered or tunnel-vision fashion. The practice of praying the Daily Office not only makes time and space for God in the mornings and evenings, but it allows time for our souls to settle and helps us see the bigger picture.

Any and all pastoral ministry must operate out of a place of stability in which the soul is settled. For me to minister to you I must first be aware of my state of being, my emotions, my identity in Christ. As Ewan Kelly puts it, 'Unless we are aware, to some degree, of what and who we are, how much of the other are we really going to see, hear, feel or understand?'[7] In order to 'see, hear, feel or understand' where other people are coming from we must first still our souls. When and only when we slow down are we capable of 'tending to the soul' of a congregation by 'coming alongside'.[8] Much of pastoral care consists of this posture of proximity, this journeying with. It is not necessarily about having the right words or 'the answer' – often we will have neither – instead it is about simply *being with*. And in this literal and figurative adjacent positioning of the self, being present to the other demands an intentional and focused slowing of our pace.

Often in pastoral situations there is an element of 'waiting with' as a person or group of people struggle with some ineffably challenging circumstance.[9] The limbo of sitting at a hospital bedside in that painfully uncertain in-between time, the despair of parents when the life-support machine is turned off, the doldrums of grief – these are deeply unsettling situations. 'Waiting with' in such scenarios requires us to lean into our settled sense of self as we seek to embody the compassion and love of Christ in that moment by actively *being alongside*.[10] We do not really need to *do* anything, but we do need to *be* that prayerful attentive presence.

It should be self-evident but to exercise effective pastoral leadership we will regularly need to go out of our way to make a difference. As in the story of the good Samaritan, responding to the needy requires 'going to' in order to come alongside and this in turn means a willingness for our plans to change somewhat. *Worthy things* sitting in our in-tray will just have to wait. Our so-called 'priorities' will find themselves reordered by compassion. The good Samaritan is not content merely to stop and tend the wounded man by the roadside. Sidelining his own plans he looks after the patient in the inn, and then proceeds to put in place a complete care package, and at his own expense, mind.

The good Samaritan engages in pedestrian pastoring, slowing down to 'the speed of love' and going out of his way to care for the other. This, of course, is a far cry from the fast-paced *showmen* we have spoken about previously. Celebrity leaders and wannabe big shots have little time for anyone but themselves and are seldom willing to be diverted from the golden pathway of their personal agenda. In contrast, *ordinary* leaders learn to be open to interruptions and proactively make time for others. There may be two dozen tasks loudly jostling for position on the 'to-do' list, but *ordinary* leaders patiently block out the noise and insist on putting people first. Jesus always made time for people and in our *unspectacular* leadership paradigm people always take precedence over tasks. Lest we forget, sharing the love of Christ with others and caring for people is *the* primary task of the Christian leader. The words of the Ordinal for the ordination of priests in the Church of England are fairly emphatic in this vein, insisting that priests are called to 'support the weak, defend the poor, and intercede for all in need'.[11]

Pursuing *unsensational* preaching

For celebrity church leaders and wannabe stars on a power trip the pulpit is a platform from which to court popularity. In the *spectacular* leadership paradigm explored previously, the sermon presents an opportunity both to showboat and to show who is boss. Watch out for the hullabaloo of energetic sentimental preaching, slogan-laden hype, rousing buzzwords and self-referential grandstanding. Watch out, because it is easy to get caught up in the moment, easy to be carried along by the emotive tones of the all-singing, all-dancing preacher-man! The pull of the charming speaker can be irresistible, and like the hapless surfer unknowingly caught in the riptide, one can be swept out to sea by seductive and sensational-sounding sophistry.

Where the preacher is ultra-emotional it often follows that they are ultra-low on content. Under the surface, *showmen* leaders tend to serve up half-baked sermons in a proof-texting pudding lightly garnished with platitudes: *tasty*, perhaps, but lacking in any sort of lasting spiritual nourishment! A nice phrase in the Portuguese language well describes such sermons as *água com açucar* – sugary water. A message, in other words, wholly lacking in substance but abundantly generous in sugar-coated soundbites. A message intended to increase the feel-good factor of the congregation by giving them what they *want* to hear but not so much the gospel truths they *need* to hear. On account of the paucity of actual scriptural teaching, these frothy offerings take effect as a sort of spiritual placebo. Overall, such sermons amount to thinly veiled self-help talks with a marked absence of biblical exegesis exacerbated by an embarrassing excess of 'spiritual' veneer. That veneer is buffed up in the polished delivery of the charismatic frontman who speaks slickly like a smiling salesman.

It is perhaps a statement of the obvious to say that such sensationalist preaching only superficially points to Christ, and that normally speaking it rather points away from him. Peel away the wafer-thin layer of saccharine oratory and it is plain that the sensational preacher preaches *self*. As countless celebrity-leader scandals have revealed, a rock and roll-style rhetoric can mask a rock and roll-style mess backstage. The wordology might be winsome but where manipulative and narcissistic leaders are at work the message will ultimately be shown up to be self-serving. Whereas John the Baptist cried, 'Forget about me, look to Jesus!' (to paraphrase John 3.30), for the *showmen* and the egocentrics the hyper-emotional supercharged sermon is really all about the preacher.

But *sensational* preaching that seeks to make a big splash does not always take on the guise of the excessively emotional electric delivery. It is not only the snazzily dressed smooth-talking celebrity types who are inclined to employ a form of preaching that is ultimately more about themselves than about the gospel of Christ. In both theologically conservative and theologically liberal contexts (interpret these labels as you will) there is a self-aggrandizing form of preaching that goes hand in hand with another sort of charisma. Here the emphasis is more cerebral than emotional, the tone *academic* rather than pastoral. Maybe like me you have found yourself scratching your head as you sit through ultra-intellectual preaching that resembles an inaugural lecture in lexicography as the congregation are ushered mercilessly into a formidable entanglement of theological watchwords and Greek mumbo jumbo!

Frankly, if preaching is an exercise in communication, and more specifically the communication of the gospel, then recourse to a highfalutin, super-intellectual style that only a professor would stand a chance of understanding is surely self-defeating. I am reminded of two things simultaneously: first, the comment – possibly apocryphal – of the South American churchgoer, 'Great sermon, what a preacher! I didn't understand a word he said, but didn't he speak beautifully!' Second, the blunt assessment of the great nineteenth-century preacher C. H. Spurgeon, who seems to have implied that the preacher who speaks to ordinary people with fancy theological words acts like an idiot.[12] Confession time: I have actually been *that guy.* Twenty-five years ago straight out of theological college I preached a sermon that blended my latest findings on an obscure phrase of biblical Hebrew with Kierkegaard's 'infinite qualitative difference'. Predictably, that sermon went down like a lead balloon (thankfully) never to be resurrected or revisited!

As I found out to my chagrin, it is ironic and (oxy)moronic that the ultra-intellectual approach to preaching, while sounding grandiose and sublimely clever, is ultimately an exercise in stupidity insofar as intellectualizing for intellectualizing's sake tends to complicate and compromise communication, rather than facilitate it. But for the power-posturing sensationalist preacher the gospel is of course secondary, for *appearing clever* and exquisitely *learned* is the foremost concern. As Lancelot Andrewes pointed out nearly 500 years ago, preachers need to be mindful that it is the 'piety of [their] prayers' and not the 'eloquence of [their] speech' that is the secret to life-transforming preaching.[13]

In addition to cerebral and overly intellectual sermonizing, we have all heard preachers whose homily is ultra-anecdotal and an exercise in painfully laboured storytelling. In essence the sermon comprises a peripatetic meandering through the various life events and 'thoughts for the day' that the preacher has recently experienced. This type of preaching can come about through a lack of preparedness or – where *showmen* stalk the stage – it is more an ode to self and a studious listing of all the great things the preacher has achieved! Ultra-anecdotal preaching makes for hard listening insofar as it strings stories together in a generally unsystematic and confusing fashion with dubitable relevance. While the preacher may be well-meaning they are unable to convey their meaning well, and the succession of stories and nice 'thoughts' have little if any synchronicity or meaningful connection to Scripture. Ultimately, it is difficult to know where such preaching is headed as it goes around the houses and around the block, and like an aircraft circling and circling without coming in to land – those stuck on the plane become increasingly frustrated![14]

Whether the preacher is ultra-emotional and ultimately vapid, ultra-intellectual and virtually unintelligible or ultra-anecdotal and largely irrelevant, preaching that seeks to leave its mark on the congregation in these ways is actually missing the mark. Waffle is waffle, whether it is well-meaning waffle, woefully self-referential waffle, wannabe intellectual waffle or genuinely ultra-intelligent waffle! Importantly, it all seems to be a far cry from the spirit of preaching that emerges in the pages of the New Testament itself. Indeed, the following is taken straight out of the preaching textbook of the guy who is arguably Christianity's greatest preacher:

> When I came to you, brothers and sisters, I did not come proclaiming the mystery of God to you in lofty words or wisdom. For I decided to know nothing among you except Jesus Christ, and him crucified. And I came to you in weakness and in fear and in much trembling. My speech and my proclamation were not with plausible words of wisdom, but with a demonstration of the Spirit and of power, so that your faith might rest not on human wisdom but on the power of God. (1 Corinthians 2.1–5)

If we wish to avoid the self-gratifying sensationalism of the *showman* and the self-satisfied intellectualism of the 'know it all' academic, we should take a leaf out of the apostle's book. *Unsensational* preaching is preaching that builds people up so that their faith 'rests not on human wisdom but on the power of God'. It is preaching that points away from self and directs people back to Jesus. Moreover, like the best sort of pastoral practice, it is preaching that seeks to *come alongside* and to *walk with* the people of God. Thus, unlike the plastic prosperity preacher or the bullying narcissistic pastor who lambast and censure their congregation from on high, the *unsensational* preacher identifies with the people of God and the sermon is as much for him or her as it is for everyone else.

The sort of preaching espoused by *ordinary* leaders is preaching preceded by prayer, preaching informed by the concerns and realities of pastoral ministry, and preaching that seeks to apply biblical teaching to everyday life. It is preaching soaked thoroughly in the balms of grace, preaching centred on the 'steadfast love' and faithfulness of God, preaching that is 'in step' with God's Spirit. It spurns any temptation to self-promote or to *sermonize* in holier than thou judgmentalism, seeking instead to offer a vista of the Kingdom through the lens of the cross and the beautifully vacant tomb. *Unsensational* preaching is never accusatory and never a pretext to corral a congregation into doing the preacher's bidding; rather it is invitational, drawing hearers back to the way of Christ and freely offering the freedom of the gospel.

In addition to content, the tone and pitch of our sermons can be significant so we need to pay attention to how we are coming across. Whereas *showmen* tend to go for hype, parading up and down while whipping people up into emotional frenzy, *unsensational* preaching refuses to be reduced to theatrics. That is not to say that the preaching we advocate is lukewarm or coldly devoid of emotion, but it will not be reduced to some vainglorious form of religious entertainment. Again, whereas the preaching of the narcissistic bully will at times come across as defensive, accusatory in tone and rant-like, *unsensational* preaching is the opposite in that it is open, undefended, hortatory and – even when animated – reassuringly serene.

Quick recap

Authentically Christian leadership takes a pedestrian approach to pastoral ministry. Since people are the priority, *ordinary leaders* make a concerted effort to come alongside and to walk with others. After the fashion of the good Samaritan, *ordinary* leaders will see and 'go to' the needy, allowing their own plans to be sidelined in the interests of compassion. That steady resolve to walk and wait with a person in need necessitates a conscious slowing down and a stilling of the self. In our *unspectacular* leadership paradigm, ministers minister out of a place of settled self-awareness, embodying a pastoral presence and a peace that is grounded in the rhythms of daily prayer. The same is true of the style of preaching that we have termed *unsensational* in that it eschews a grandstanding, ultra-emotional or ultra-intellectual approach, opting instead for unostentatious gospel communication characterized by grace.

Questions for reflection

1 Are there any measures you need to take in your own life and leadership in order to slow down so as to come alongside others more effectively?

2 What opportunities might there be in your own context to 'go to' the needy and show them the compassion of Christ?

3 Reflect on your own experience of preaching and/or speaking in front of others. Is there anything that you might do differently to improve your communication in the light of what you have read in this chapter?

Notes

1 Bonhoeffer, D., 1996, *The Cost of Discipleship*, London: SCM, pp. 29–30.

2 Koyama, K., 1979, *Three Mile an Hour God*, London: SCM, p. 8.

3 Ibid.

4 Morris, L., 1988, *Luke*, Leicester: InterVarsity Press, p. 207.

5 Collicutt, J., 2015, *The Psychology of Christian Character Formation*, London: SCM, p. 184.

6 Ibid.

7 Kelly, E., 2012, *Personhood and Presence: Self as a Resource for Spiritual and Pastoral Care*, New York: Bloomsbury, p. 3.

8 Trible, J. L. (Sr), 2005, *Transformative Pastoral Leadership in the Black Church*, New York: Palgrave Macmillan, pp. 10–11.

9 Kelly, *Personhood and Presence*, pp. 28–9, 31.

10 Ibid.

11 Throup, M., 2022, *When Jesus Calls*, Norwich: Canterbury Press, p. 119.

12 Spurgeon, C. H., 1960, *An All-Round Ministry*, London: The Banner of Truth Trust, p. 44.

13 Newman, J. H. and Neale, J. M., trans., 1957, *The Private Prayers of Lancelot Andrewes*, London: SCM, p. 105.

14 In a widely used analogy the introduction of a sermon is comparable to take-off whereas the conclusion is comparable to landing a plane. For a practical guide on crafting a sermon with a worked example, see Throup, M., 2022, *Preaching Beyond the Pandemic*, Nottingham: Grove, pp. 19–24.

PART 3

A viable leadership pattern

7

Wellbeing and *being* well
(caring for self)

Our need for belonging has a broader horizon. We need to be-
long to a larger purpose. We need a reason to live and a frame-
work that makes sense of all that has happened. We need a
sense that our life matters. (Carla A. Grosch Miller)[1]

Our ability to confront the aspects of our character that risk
our coming off the rails and leading us (and those we lead) to
harm and failure is key to our success and finding authenticity.
(Lisa Oakley and Justin Humphreys)[2]

There is a modern myth that has plagued Western society for
the past few decades and that is the notion of a 'healthy work–
life balance'. This seemingly innocuous phrase is in fact riddled
with difficulties. For a start, what do we mean by 'healthy', and
who gets to decide what 'healthy' looks like for one person or
another? How in good conscience can we speak of 'balance'
in a society awash with zero hour contracts, housing crises
and people around us suffering from fuel poverty and even
going hungry – and this in a wealthy nation such as the UK, to
say nothing of the wider world? Sure, we all know what this
phrase is *aiming at*, what it is *trying to say* and what it is *trying*
to achieve. However, in a world still reeling from an epoch-
defining pandemic, work and life are increasingly pressured and
even for those of us blessed enough to have stable jobs and
domestic security, most of the time any semblance of equilibrium is a rather risible pipe dream.

Within Christian ministry and leadership there is another
unrealistic but very real myth that undermines any sense of

work–life 'balance'. This is that the leader should be available for all and sundry 24/7 and twice on Sundays! The nature of Christian leadership is of course *diakonia* – service, but when did this ever equate to working oneself to a premature death? In a volume on former Church of England bishops, Trevor Beeson observes how several of the Victorian and early twentieth-century episcopal bench effectively worked themselves to an early grave.[3] Again, George Herbert is an iconic and much-celebrated priest and poet-theologian, but his penchant for overwork and unremitting activism sits uneasily alongside his sustained ill health and untimely death after just three years in parish ministry.[4] Four hundred years later, we know that dangerous patterns of overwork are still very much a feature of life for many in Christian leadership. But it really should not be this way.

Nowadays we talk a lot about wellbeing in ministry, largely because we are struggling to achieve it. One of the reasons currently mentioned in connection with the drop in numbers of those coming forward for ordination in the Church of England is the lack of stability and the increasingly pressured nature of the priestly role.[5] People speak of the 'crisis of wellbeing in ministry', and in the Anglican context there is the 'Covenant for Clergy Care and Wellbeing', which is designed to protect ordained ministers – mostly from themselves.[6] In Christian leadership we should all have those to whom we are accountable, i.e. those who are tasked with caring for us as leaders. Ensuring that this is the case is perhaps a primary feature of good self-care. And it is a commitment to self-care that enables *ordinary* leaders to go about God's business of caring for others in a sustainable and responsible way.

In Chapter 6 we referred to Jesus' Parable of the Good Samaritan and speculated that the Samaritan is a practitioner of *unspectacular* leadership, the type of leadership that goes out of its way to care for others, putting the interests of those in need above any self-interest. However, in a perceptive piece of feminist theology titled 'The Self-Differentiated Samaritan', Jeanne Stevenson-Moessner draws attention to a neglected dimension of the parable.[7] Namely, that the Samaritan completed his journey. While his care for his neighbour is commonly commended, we should also note that he 'loved himself'.[8] Building on Moessner's observations, we can see that with recourse to a team effort (the inn and its host) the Samaritan resists the temptation to go it alone and to derail his own wellbeing. In this way, therefore, Jesus' Good Samaritan paradigm 'supports the notion that in genuine caretaking the caretaker is not submerged'.[9]

In my role as a mentor to those who are preparing for ministry within the Church of England and other churches I often encounter people who I fear may end up getting *submerged*. I marvel at the many missional things our students are involved in, whether it is visiting offenders in prison, setting up food banks, leading small groups or pastorally supporting refugees, but I *worry* that while taking care of others our emerging leaders can fail to take care of self. People who put themselves forward for leadership within the church tend to be those who have a huge heart for others. But having a heart for others does not mean neglecting your own heart! It is tragic when Christian leaders become casualties of their own compassionate zeal and struggle to *complete the journey* because of physical, emotional and spiritual exhaustion.

Therefore, to prevent overwork from becoming the default and to guard against the closely associated *doormat syndrome* – where church leaders are walked over by those who always take a mile when given an inch – there has to be a studied intentionality around self-care. While I suspect that in the complex world we inhabit it may ultimately be unrealistic to talk about a 'healthy work–life balance', it is vital that we take our 'wellbeing' seriously. There *are* proactive steps that we can take to ensure that we ourselves find shelter and hospitality as we provide them for others. Part of this is the discipline of embedding those rhythms and routines that will help the 'caretaker' complete their journey, and this is something we will touch on below.

A word on wellbeing and exercising *ruthless* self-care

I am drawn to the slightly tongue in cheek notion of the 'unbusy pastor' mooted by Eugene Peterson some years ago.[10] In cautioning against the tendency of Christian leaders to overwork and overstretch themselves with a thousand and one things, Peterson advocates a *back to basics* approach not unlike the *unspectacular* leadership paradigm and the 'pedestrian pastoring' idea explored here in earlier chapters. A key observation is that Christian leaders can sometimes allow others to set the agenda for them and thus become busied with this, that and the other – activities that are not necessarily priorities or the right things to be focusing on.[11] If this is something that sounds familiar then there is a pressing need to wrest back control of your own diary and (to the degree that this is possible) do due diligence on delegating and distributing tasks within the team.

Over the years I have learnt to become *ruthless* in the exercise of self-care. You have to. If you want to complete the journey in one piece there can be no messing about with your own wellbeing. Forward planning and diary work is one factor in the preservation of self. The importance of blocking out time in your schedule for rest, recovery, retreat, study and family is well known but unless you actually sit down and *proactively* diarize your time out and ring-fence your time off this can slip. After a gruellingly long and intense day before, I can tell you that these days I have absolutely no qualms about taking an extended *siesta* the day after. Sure, it is not always possible – once again, the work–life balance equation is seldom wholly soluble – but an intentionality around ring-fencing rest makes it possible *sometimes*.

Now *ruthless* self-care does entail learning to mute the internal voice that bangs on about those things that one 'would, could and should' be doing. Most Christian leaders are disinclined to switch off even temporarily and it is not necessarily easy to re-educate and reprogramme ourselves when it comes to caring for self. I wince now as I think back to the three-year period in my life when I struggled horrendously with a chronic back issue. The crippling pain was pretty much constant but on recollection, I stubbornly refused to take even a day off work during that time until I finally went in for spinal surgery. Colleagues would regularly find me lying on the floor of the diocesan office grimacing in pain as I tackled paperwork from a prone position! Alas, a misshapen sense of duty together with a misplaced sense of pride can lead us to become so stubbornly task-focused that we fail even to use our common sense about self-preservation.

Elsewhere I have written about the necessity of establishing rhythms and routines that ground and sustain leaders for a life in Christian ministry.[12] It is not my intention to copy and paste that material here but once more I want to emphasize the need to be *ruthless* about sticking to those spiritual routines and rhythms of life. This is not only about *spiritual* disciplines and the prayer life – it is about time with friends, time by myself and time *away* from all the church stuff. Again, if you find that the routine is slipping or that you are losing rhythm then *diarize* those vital appointments that help you relax and recharge. The road to burnout is paved with good intentions: don't just think about blocking out rest periods – get hold of your diary and block them out!

Theologically, the kind of self-care exercised by *ordinary* leaders is enshrined within what is often referred to as the 'Sabbath principle'. To this day, the Jewish Sabbath exemplifies a *ruthless* uncompromising imperative to rest. Some years ago in Jerusalem I watched as a hotel manager paced out the route between the elevator and the foyer, taking careful measurements to help the staff observe the Sabbath by not walking more than the permitted distance during that window of time. It is interesting that the biblical account suggests that on the Sabbath God *mandates* rest and prohibits work – seemingly we need that strong double steer! Unexpectedly, perhaps, God *blesses* this rest day, that is, God blesses a period of time. This is an unusual detail since God tends to bless living beings that they may bear fruit, something that in turn suggests a connection between rest and fruitfulness.[13]

It is worth just exploring that connection for a moment. In a helpful book called *Sabbath Rest*, my colleague Mark Scarlata explains that the blessing of time is what actually sustains creation and allows it to keep pouring forth its produce.[14] For Scarlata, the divine pattern of 'blessing and ceasing' is what maintains the life cycle of the world.[15] The same can be said of humanity and – lest we forget – without Sabbath not only do we become unproductive but our lives 'quickly deteriorate into endless activity, anxiety, stress, fear and exhaustion'.[16] Ultimately, if God is somewhat radical in his approach to rest, then there is no excuse for Christian leaders to pursue patterns of *restlessness*. Instead, our lives as *ordinary* leaders must be conformed to that divine pattern of 'blessing and ceasing' and we must *ruthlessly* procure rest. Naturally, the busier we become, the more *ruthless* we will need to become about rest and self-care!

Being well as the prerequisite of our *wellbeing*

While the foregoing section provides one or two practical pointers that will aid *ordinary* leaders to look out for their own wellbeing in the day-to-day grind, here we take a step back to talk about *being* well. In order to address fully the issue of 'wellbeing' in ministry there has to be a parallel conversation about *being* well. This isn't just a tongue twister or empty rhetoric. *Being* well is the necessary precursor of wellbeing. *Being* well is about a fundamental conviction concerning the purpose and sense of our existence in a world that often makes little sense. Within that there is a component pertaining to self-understanding and an acceptance of what it means to be human under the God of grace.

To pick up on the quotation from Carla Grosch Miller at the head of the chapter, within a Christian worldview *being* well is ultimately about *belonging*. Knowing that I am created *imago Dei* and that I am not here on account of some grand cosmological coincidence but that I have a place within the created order helps make sense of where *I fit in* to it all. Moreover, the knowledge that I and indeed all human life is the precious object of the love of God assures me at the most basic level that 'life matters' and that *my* life matters. Taking things further, the revelation of God in the person of Jesus Christ – with the wonderful promise of salvation and life in him – gives me a greater appreciation of the meaning and value of our life as human beings under God and our eschatological potential for flourishing. Anchored in a biblical creation theology, it is this sort of theological anthropology – or, in Luke Bretherton's reworking, theological *ecology* – that provides the fundamental framework within which meaning and purpose begin to emerge as we perceive that we *belong* to God in Christ, to one another and to the created order.[17]

This sense of *belonging* creates the conditions for us to live an integrated and fruitful life. That said, there are forces at work both within us and externally that disrupt and disturb our existence. Rather than deny or downplay the chaotic and more negative elements that impinge on our human character we must regularly step back to reflect on ourselves in an honest and constructive way. Our *being* well as Christians and particularly as Christian leaders is not automatic or something to be taken for granted. On the one hand there is a constant daily need to go back to the well and receive the water of life from the Lord of life himself. On the other, there is a periodic need to take time out and really listen in to our life and tune in to what is going on within us. With the help of a slightly unusual and apocryphal story we shall attempt to do this below!

Being well as we come face to face with our shadow

The apocryphal Gospels might not be your favourite bedtime reading and that word 'apocryphal' suggests they are a bit dodgy! Nevertheless, they do contain some charming albeit most probably fictitious takes on Jesus' early life as well as some fairly weird and wacky stuff straight out of left-field! One legendary story that I really like comes from the *Infancy Gospel of Thomas* and reports how a rather inept Joseph manages to mess up his woodwork. Somehow he miscalculates so that the dimensions of the bed he is making end up all wrong. A piece of wood has been cut too short, something that can't easily be remedied! I can imagine Joseph – that paragon of virtue as per his profile in the Gospel of Matthew – revealing something of his shadow side, perhaps quietly effing and blinding in Aramaic under his breath. A first-class blunder: what on earth can he do to sort this one out? Wood is costly, and this is a costly error. Thankfully all is not lost. The boy Jesus assesses the situation and without further ado miraculously stretches the curtailed plank so that it becomes the correct length! In a twenty-first-century parallel, I note that my own children can themselves perform similar miracles when I can't get my smartphone to do the things I need it to do.

While the purpose of the story is doubtless to draw attention to the divine nature of the boy Jesus, I am drawn to the humanness of the man Joseph. Since I am technically challenged and most of the time struggle to put together even a simple flatpack, it is quite reassuring that an experienced handyman like Joseph can get things so badly wrong! Christian leadership books regularly appeal to scriptural leaders and heroes of the faith, encouraging us to emulate their example. In some of these publications the foibles and de facto failings of biblical leaders tend to be held up as reminders that we are all fallible. And yet, as Christian leaders we insist on talking a good game. Even in the tougher times we pretend that we are somehow OK when we are really not OK. It is as if there were some faith or doctrinal requirement for us to be completely with it, unflappable, invulnerable and perfectly together 24/7.

At a low-key church event I recall introducing a colleague to a pastor I had once worked with. Said pastor proceeded to talk my colleague through the intricacies and contours of their ministerial CV in a *tour de force* of name-dropping that lasted well over ten minutes. Anyone would think that this was a job interview rather than a casual conversation with a stranger at a social event! But this behaviour pattern is very much one I recognize. I have most definitely been *that guy.* I hope that this is not the case, but I suspect that on occasion I can still be *that guy* (if you ever meet me and find me being *that guy*, please send me straight back to this paragraph without passing go!).

But this is not necessarily the arrogance of a *showman* at work. When leaders default to parroting their achievements – where they studied and under whom, successes chalked up, significant events they were invited to – this is often a defence mechanism rooted in feelings of insecurity.

In *The Emotionally Healthy Leader* Pete Scazzero offers some insightful thoughts on the 'shadow' in leadership. We all possess a shadow, this being 'the accumulation of untamed emotions, less-than-pure motives and thoughts that, while largely uncon-scious, strongly influence and shape your behaviors'.[18] Derived from psychology, the notion of the 'shadow' is somewhat elusive and should not be equated straightforwardly with sin. Scazzero explains that while certain elements of our shadow may be sinful, the shadow is also about weaknesses and wounds acquired over time. Typically, aspects of the shadow manifest in mechanisms of self-defence when an individual feels vulnerable, threatened or exposed.[19]

As the name suggests, elements of the shadow tend to be negative or undesirable traits that often equate to the flip side of a positive characteristic. Thus, a gifted Christian leader may be able to encourage and inspire others with their words, but their shadow may manifest in self-referential posturing that in turn betrays a need to be affirmed and accepted. Again, Scazzero lists some instructive examples of where the shadow reveals itself in leadership. For example, valuing excellence (a good thing) can reveal a shadow side of perfectionism. A zeal for God's truth and right doctrine can sometimes lead to a fearful-ness and lack of love shown towards people taking a different view.[20] I would add that in Christian leadership a positive drive to serve and give 100 per cent to God and the people you are called to serve can reveal a shadow of overwork, dependence on self and unhealthy activism.

Being well requires us to recognize and own our humanness. If even a paragon of virtue like Joseph can get his measure-ments all wrong, requiring Jesus to put things right, the same is very much true for me! The song we sing with children in church is 'Jesus you're my superhero', but thankfully *I* am not called to be some kind of superhero or superhuman minister.

Thank goodness for that! In life and in leadership it takes courage to recognize our humanity and our human vulnerability. It certainly takes courage to come face to face with our shadow and seek awareness of behaviours and tendencies within us that are unhealthy and unhelpful. But this is something we need to do prayerfully and in the power of God's Spirit if we want to get on the road to wellbeing, and to exercise effective self-care. Returning to our *unspectacular* leadership paradigm, *ordinary* leaders tend to be people who regularly and prayerfully confront their shadow.

Now this isn't about beating ourselves up over our inadequacies, shortcomings or day-to-day failures to achieve *holiness*. As Martin Luther eventually discovered, there is no place for self-flagellation within a worldview rebooted by the gospel of grace. Confronting the shadow is more a coming to terms with our inbuilt vulnerability and the refusal to deny or repress the existence of impulses that are part and parcel of our natural life. We know that it is damaging when, for example, thoughts of anger, lust, self-loathing, the desire for recognition or a thirst for vengeance are denied, internalized or locked down. In some cases the denial and repression of emotions emerging from the shadow can ultimately erupt to the surface in abusive behaviour. On the flip side, where such elements are acknowledged, identified and accepted as part of the human experience, we can deal with them better, seek the transformative grace of God, and learn how to live without becoming ensnared by secretive inner fears and pessimistic self-condemnatory thoughts.[21]

Thus, over time, by facing up to or facing down their shadow, *ordinary* leaders grow in self-knowledge, self-acceptance and a healthy love of self. The acknowledgement of our limitations and the choice, paraphrasing Paul Tillich, to accept that while in some ways *unacceptable*, God accepts and loves us all the same, is an immensely freeing decision. The net result of this are leaders who become steadily more secure in themselves as they stand in Christ, demonstrating a balanced sense of self-worth and self-esteem. Such *ordinary* leaders tend to demonstrate the quality of 'trustworthiness' found in the Church of England's Formational Framework because they are realistic and open about both their strengths and their vulnerabilities and increasingly dependent on the grace of God.

It follows, therefore, that Christian leaders flourish where there is a robust biblically informed framework for *being* well, a framework that helps situate each person within the 'ecology of mutual blessing', to cite Bretherton once more.[22] Rooted in a sense of self-acceptance deriving from their identity in Christ, *ordinary* leaders can then go to work on their *wellbeing* and in turn ensure the *wellbeing* of others. As discussed in the earlier part of the chapter, in practical terms personal *wellbeing* is as much a series of proactive choices as it is a state of mind. These choices involve exercising kindness towards self and ensuring that there is no compromise when it comes to what I am terming '*ruthless* self-care'.

Quick recap

While 'wellbeing' is something of a buzzword and a popular topic in society as well as in church, *being* well is the precondition of *wellbeing*. A rigorously biblical theological anthropology that affirms the value of all human life as well as of each individual human life is central to *being* well. The self-acceptance and appropriate confidence conferred by a knowledge of the saving grace of Jesus and an identity located in Christ enable *ordinary* leaders to take a realistic, rounded and non-condemnatory, non-defeatist view of themselves. With courage and guided by the Holy Spirit, such leaders confront their 'shadow' reassured that in God's peculiar logic 'strength is made perfect in weakness'. Thus, seeking to become more and more Christ-like, *ordinary* leaders appreciate the absolute necessity to take time out and time off because caring for others demands taking care of self and care of others will falter where self-care is neglected. *Wellbeing* is not to be trifled with. Rather, all Christian leaders must take a *ruthless* uncompromising approach to the priority of self-care.

Questions for reflection

1 To what extent might it be true that any discussion of *well-being* necessitates some parallel thinking about *being* well?

2 What is the 'shadow' and why is it important for *ordinary* leaders to be aware of their shadow and to confront it from time to time?

3 What steps might you need to take to become more *ruthless* in regard to self-care and ensuring your own *wellbeing*?

Notes

1 Grosch Miller, C. A., 2021, *Trauma and Pastoral Care: A Ministry Handbook*, Norwich: Canterbury Press, p. 155.

2 Oakley, L. and Humphreys, J., 2019, *Escaping the Maze of Spiritual Abuse: Creating Healthy Christian Cultures*, London: SPCK, pp. 125–6.

3 Beeson, T., 2002, *The Bishops*, London: SCM, pp. 50, 59, 124, 127.

4 While the memory of George Herbert is generally lauded in Anglican circles, some have questioned the wisdom of using his short and frenetic term as a country vicar as a prototype for modern ministry. See Lewis-Anthony, J., 2009, *If You Meet George Herbert on the Road, Kill Him: Radically Rethinking Priestly Ministry*, London: Mowbray.

5 Private communication from a senior member within the Church of England, but this line of reasoning is no secret and is mentioned regularly in social media threads about declining vocations to ordained ministry.

6 This is available for download via www.churchofengland.org, the Church of England website.

7 Stevenson-Moessner, J., 2005, 'The Self-Differentiated Samaritan', in Dykstra, R. C., ed., 2005, *Images of Pastoral Care: Classic Readings*, St Louis, MO: Chalice Press, pp. 62–8.

8 Ibid, p. 66.

9 Ibid, p. 66.

10 Peterson, E. H., 1989, *The Contemplative Pastor*, Dallas, TX: Word, pp. 27–34.

11 Ibid, p. 29. Cf. Aisthorpe, S., 2020, *Rewilding the Church*, Edinburgh: St Andrew Press, pp. 160–8, who also references Peterson's well-known imagery in his cautioning against the 'noxious impact of the frenetic'.

12 See Throup, M., 2022, *When Jesus Calls*, Norwich: Canterbury Press.

13 See Wilkinson, D., 2002, *The Message of Creation*, Nottingham: InterVarsity Press, p. 44.

14 Scarlata, M., 2019, *Sabbath Rest: The Beauty of God's Rhythm for a Digital Age*, London: SCM, pp. 46–7.

15 Ibid, p. 47.

16 Ibid.

17 Bretherton, L., 2023, *A Primer in Christian Ethics: Christ and the Struggle to Live Well*, Cambridge: Cambridge University Press, pp. 42–4.

18 Scazzero, P., 2015, *The Emotionally Healthy Leader*, Grand Rapids, MI: Zondervan, p. 55. For more on the 'shadow' in relation to pastoral ministry, see Kelly, E., 2012, *Personhood and Presence: Self as a Resource for Spiritual and Pastoral Care*, New York: Bloomsbury, pp. 67–70.

19 Ibid.

20 Ibid, p. 56.

21 This paragraph draws on some of the thinking found in Bloomfield, I., 1978, '*Religion and Psychotherapy: Friends or Foes?*', pp. 117–26; and specifically in Willows, D. and Swinton, J., eds, 2000, *Spiritual Dimensions of Pastoral Care: Practical Theology in a Multidisciplinary Context*, London: Jessica Kingsley, p.124.

22 Bretherton, L., 2023, *A Primer in Christian Ethics: Christ and the Struggle to Live Well*, Cambridge: Cambridge University Press, p. 40.

8

Curating places of grace (caring for self and others)

How very good and pleasant it is when kindred live together in unity! (Psalm 133.1)

The responsibility that is on the shoulders of leaders in the church to guide, teach and preach in ways that do not harm others is possibly one of the greatest ... Our mission is towards a safer church that encourages personal (and not necessarily numerical) growth, flourishing and a greater knowledge of who God is for the good of all. (Justin Humphreys)[1]

As a keen angler it is heartbreaking for me to come across watery places that have been contaminated by pollutants. The sight of fish floating helplessly on a grimy surface, desperate for oxygen, evokes a sense of righteous anger. How did things become so toxic here? In what is supposed to be a thriving environment teeming with life the creatures that call this place home are struggling to breathe, stifled and suffocated by noxious substances that should be nowhere near this place. How did the relevant authorities allow things to get this bad? Who is going to come in and clean up the mess and revive the ecosystem? Will those responsible be held to account and, vitally, how can we prevent this from happening again?

Tragically, in church organizations where *showmen* self-identify as the big fish of the little pond, toxic subcultures stifle and damage the sacred habitat. An ecclesial environment that would otherwise be alive with God's Spirit can become poisoned by censorship, forced accountability and manipulative machinations. In heavily rule-based cultish church communities a narrow and hermeneutically suspect biblical fundamentalism cuts off the spiritual oxygen supply as control-freak pastors obsess about 'purity' and prevent people from mixing with 'outsiders'. The corrosive effects of coercive control, passive aggression, suppression, gaslighting and petty one-upmanship are tantamount to spiritual suffocation. Bullying behaviour and an interfering *do as I say* (but not as I do) form of pharisaic legalism muddies the waters and contaminates the soul. With recourse to the pseudo-spiritual tropes of *spectacular* leader-ship, spiritually abusive leaders guilt-trip the congregation about not *doing enough*, not *giving enough*, not *being holy enough*. Stuck on repeat, the invective and judgmentalism of heavy-shepherding leaders act like toxins on the body of Christ in a given locale. Once more we find ourselves asking how those in authority allowed things to get so bad. Who will come and clean up the mess and revive the ecclesial ecosystem? Will those responsible be held to account, and, vitally, how might we prevent this kind of thing from happening again?

It should go without saying that appropriate care in the aftermath of abuse is vitally important, though numerous docu-mentaries and reports suggest that churches and parachurch organizations have not always got this right.[2] Again, to state what should be obvious, it is essential that victims of church-based abuse or those who suspect they might be victims of such abuse are taken seriously, listened to, supported and cared for by professionals, and that the appropriate authorities take responsibility and action to ensure that this happens in a timely way. Equally, perpetrators of church-based abuse must be held to account and receive appropriate support as they are con-fronted with the harm that their actions have caused others. In what follows our focus will be on that final question, i.e. how might we prevent a toxic culture of spiritual abuse from taking hold in organizations that bear the name of Christ?

To answer this question we begin by acknowledging that as Christian leaders we have the potential and the power to shape an environment positively or negatively. As we will explore below, the manner in which we speak and act goes a long way towards determining the general feel of a place. Thus, when *ordinary* leaders adopt an open, undefended and generous approach, spiritual oxygen enters the ecclesial ecosystem. *Unspectacular* leadership operates on the basis of an inclusive, invitational, mutually affirming and non-judgmental stance, a stance that allows breathing space and opportunities for people to be themselves in their environment. Whereas *showmen* leaders rule with an iron fist and have no truck with questioners, *ordinary* leaders show humility and are open to challenge. Whereas coercive control-freak leaders insist stubbornly that individuals do their bidding, *ordinary* leaders offer guidance but always allow people to make their own free choices. As Justin Humphreys puts it in his reflection on Jesus' encounter with the wealthy young man in Matthew 19, 'choice is the antidote to control'.[3]

There is, undoubtedly, a close connection between a healthy stewardship of self (cf. Chapter 7) and exercising a healthy care of others. By treating ourselves generously as the recipients of divine grace we in turn are more likely to treat others with that same generosity and grace. Since attentive and appropriate self-care enables and even fuels a proper stewardship of those we are privileged to serve, it follows that in order to oxygenate our ecclesial ecosystems our own lives must first be spiritually oxygenated by the Lord and life-giver. Undoubtedly, *ordinary* leaders can be influential in creating physical environments that may be designated 'safe spaces'. However, where this multi-directional spiritual oxygenation occurs they can also become conduits of the Holy Spirit so as to shape the spiritual landscape of their environment. In this way *ordinary* leaders become curators not just of safe spaces but of places of grace.

Expunging unrealistic expectations

Once more the chief concern of this chapter is to explore how Christian leaders can curate places of grace and prevent their environments from becoming poisoned by spiritual abuse. The power and influence of the leadership in shaping the culture of the organization should not be underestimated here, so it is important to look at *how* things can go downhill if we are to prevent that from happening in our own leadership. This will mean taking a look at the ways in which ministers and church workers *arrive* in a place and bring their own perspectives into a given organization. Above all this is a discussion about *expectations* that leaders bring to ministry and what happens when these expectations are frustrated.

In Chapter 4 we did some thinking about the core expectations that are placed on ministers from a biblical perspective, but what about our own expectations of the life of leadership in ministry and what it entails? Church leadership and particularly the task of local (parish) ministry has been described by Archbishop Justin Welby as 'the hardest work I have ever done, and the most stressful', and rightly so.[4] Whatever else it might be, ministry on the ground is no walk in the park. The fact is that if you begin with a rosy caricature of ministry allied with unrealistic expectations of yourself and others, then you are headed for trouble. I have a hunch that posturing *showmen* and leaders who exhibit spiritually abusive behaviour often begin ministry optimistically on the front foot, but with overblown and unreal expectations about it all. They arrive in a place with the kind of naïve thinking that expects church growth to happen automatically, as if by magic, just by virtue of them rocking up there![5]

Problems arise when after time there is little to show in the way of tangible 'results'. Typically, frustration sets in along with a sense that 'things aren't as they should be'. It is then a short step to the sentiment that 'people aren't doing what they ought to', which can fester and fuel a misplaced sense of entitlement. Where leaders lack appropriate accountability and good mentoring, negative thoughts can translate quite quickly into unchecked sentiments of self-pity and bristling indignation. Thus, the complaint that 'things aren't as they should be' births a tacit or eventually overt 'I deserve better than this' sentiment. As negativity takes root a range of bitter feelings manifest: 'this wasn't why I entered ministry', 'it's OK for Pastor Tim down the road!', 'my congregation don't value me', 'I am in charge here, so you better get in line!' Naturally, we can all get frustrated at times, but if our framing expectations are off-piste to begin with then we are more likely to find our way onto the slippery slope that descends into unhealthy leadership and toxicity.

As someone involved in preparing people for various roles within church ministry I am concerned that we – that is, those of us with leadership responsibilities within the Church of England – are not always as clear about the character of this ministry as we could be. At the risk of sounding unduly curmudgeonly and without wishing to rain on anyone's parade, those currently in the process of exploring a vocation to public ministry should note well both the unusual and the generally *unspectacular* nature of this life. While there will be *eureka* moments of breakthrough, precious seasons of blessing and halcyon days when God works in inexplicably wondrous ways – including through you – much of ministry is more mundane and undramatic in character. Our bread and butter are the rhythms and disciplines of daily prayer, pastoral care and administration. It is important to develop and hold on to this *habitus* – the daily inhabiting of a simple, straightforward spirituality – because it is this framework that helps hold things together when the task list gets onerous and when the fireworks are damp with no obvious encouragements or particular 'results' to speak of.

To avoid the gradual downward spiral that slips from frustration to bitterness and ultimately into apathy, ill health, 'quiet quitting' and behaviours that adversely affect others, *ordinary* leaders need to set their co-ordinates for ministry in realistic and healthy ways. In my early twenties it was immensely freeing when a senior member of the South American Mission Society explained to me that during our first three-year term of mission and ministry in Brazil we should seek to get to know people, help out where possible and get involved alongside local church leaders where appropriate. Since we were not given any particular targets or a lengthy checklist of tasks we would be expected to perform, the pressure was off. As leaders we need breathing space when we arrive in a new place and the time to get established. It is unfair to be burdened by others – or indeed to burden ourselves – with unrealistic expectations and/or unfair numerical targets.

In the *unspectacular* leadership paradigm we have explored in this book, healthy ministry is primarily about *being* and not so much about *doing*. *Being* a person of integrity and faithfulness to Christ, *being* a person who stewards self wisely and *being* a person who is there for others. *Ordinary* leaders seek to curate places of grace in which others feel safe and have the freedom to encounter the love of God and express themselves freely. As for 'targets' – what about aiming at *being* a Christ-like presence in that place to which you are called? How about focusing on giving others the opportunity to be themselves so as to exercise their gifts with confidence? These are the sort of objectives Christian leaders ought to be concerned with, where the 'cure of souls' takes precedence over *counting bodies*.

Curating places of grace

Building on our discussion so far, and recognizing the power that we have as leaders, in this section we consider attitudes and actions we can embrace so as to make a difference in the creation and cultivation of spiritually healthy ecosystems. Here we ask, 'What can we be doing proactively to ensure that our church communities are spiritually healthy and safe spaces for all?' To answer this question I want to explore a range of attitudes, behaviours and actions that together provide a potent formula for the curation of places of grace. These are *reflexivity, accountability, tone-setting, creating culture, mutual responsibility* and *legacy*. This is not intended to be an exhaustive list, nor is the terminology explored here necessarily new, but again, taken together these elements provide a firm steer in the right direction.[6]

In regard to *reflexivity*, the New Testament is replete with warnings and encouragements for Christian leaders to keep a close eye on themselves and their ministry (see, for example, 1 Timothy 3.1–13). To a degree we touched on this in Chapter 7 but I make no apology for reiterating that a routine of critical self-examination ought to be hard-wired into those who occupy positions of authority and trust in the church. This, by and large, comprises a self-reflective, periodic and prayerful spiritual health check-up. Typically it will draw on searching questions such as the following: what emotions am I sensing in myself in relation to ministry and those in my care? Where are the frustrations right now, what is causing them and what might be done to mitigate these in a fair, timely and responsible manner? Where have I got it wrong, to whom might I need to apologize and to whom do I look for support? What are the true motivations and intentions behind my plans? Who is supporting *me* at this time and are my support structures adequate for the demands of ministry in this season? Are there wounds or issues arising from childhood and/or previous experiences that I need to address with a professional? Am I exercising kindness and grace to myself and being ruthless about self-care?

It is true that as Scripture teaches us the human heart is deceptive, so while clearly important, *reflexivity* will only take us so far. A genuinely reflective, undefended and open approach to the self in Christian leadership must be complemented by rigid and healthy structures of *accountability*. Not only do I need to reflect deeply about my ministry practice and its underlying motivations, but I need also to bounce this off wise counsellors, mentors and other Christian leaders who will be able to encourage and gently admonish me in a fully transparent way. Sometimes the obvious just needs stating and restating. Thus, every Christian leader should make it a top priority to diarize regular meetings of both formal accountability (i.e. line management), and more informal accountability (i.e. spiritual direction, mentoring, etc). Where regular supervision is in place, warning signs may be picked up early so that *prior to becoming problems* issues can be dealt with – in prayer, through counselling, with the support of others. Thus, where healthy accountability supplements active reflexivity, the risks of slipping into unhealthy leadership patterns are mitigated. Consequently, ministers are less likely to burn out and/or take out their frustrations and secret fears on others.

Tone-setting is a bit different from reflexivity and accountability in that it is mainly forward-looking, being outward-facing more than it is introspective. For Christian leaders, tone-setting is about making a straightforward statement of gospel intent and starting as we mean to go on. It is about clear signposting, consistent messaging and concrete actions that back up our words. To take a simple example, when a priest takes on a new parish in the Church of England they may set an 'open-door' policy by offering an open invitation for people to drop in for a chat. Matching words and actions set the tone and – since we have begun with this example – down-to-earth, accessible and approachable leadership is the kind we might expect to find from parish priests who are keen to encourage healthy, safe church cultures.

When I began as Centre Director of a theological college in London I was keen to set the right tone from the outset and after some prayerful reflection I brought in the simple strapline 'community of compassion' (which, it turns out, the Bishop of London had also introduced, so it was good to know that we were on the same page as the bishop!). It is a phrase that features in my written college communications and in my talks from the front, but more than mere words it speaks to the very *essence* of our life together and how we interact with each other. As a baseline vision of what we are seeking to become in Christ, the 'community of compassion' ethos only carries weight if my words and actions model and champion it. Folks will only catch the vision, run with it and own it if the actions and behaviours of those up front consistently set the standard in a meaningful and genuine way. Authentic tone-setting is a far cry from *spin*, where troubled and manipulative leaders deploy slick but ultimately meaningless catchphrases and buzzwords in ever more desperate attempts to paper over the cracks of failing institutions and burgeoning personal crises. Instead, it is the verbalizing and enactment of good practice and behaviour from the front that help to inculcate gospel values and foster the creation and curation of grace-filled places.

Whereas reflexivity, accountability and tone-setting relate specifically to the ministry and life of the Christian leader or to the leadership circle of a church, the remaining terms *creating culture, mutual responsibility* and *legacy* relate to the community more widely. True, as figureheads Christian leaders have a role to play in *creating culture*, but it takes a collective effort to create a healthy spiritual and safe culture within a church or parachurch organization. To return to the 'community of compassion' ethos, this becomes embedded when students and staff at the college look out for each other in appropriate and caring ways. A positive culture is created where those within the organization demonstrate its values in what they say and do. In our case, staff and students cultivate a caring community by ensuring that everyone who steps through our doors is welcomed. This is achieved by taking it in turns to serve others in particular tasks, and by showing respect to and for one another – even and especially where we hold deep disagreements on thorny theological issues! In churches the creation of a healthy and inclusive culture happens in much the same way.

Once more, we are likely to find places of grace and healthy churches where there is a sense of *mutual responsibility* in relation to the preservation and promotion of the overarching ethos and values of the institution. After a particular tone has been set and a certain type of culture created, Christian leaders will empower and encourage others so that all become aware of their role in and responsibility for maintaining a spiritually healthy and increasingly Christ-shaped community. As is the case with safeguarding more generally, so with the curating of spiritually healthy churches – this is never the responsibility of one person or the remit of a small team; rather it is incumbent on every one of us to *wear the T-shirt* and get stuck in. Again, leadership that strives for mutuality, seeking to empower others and offering appropriate levels of support and supervision, is exactly the sort of leadership we might expect to encounter in healthy churches and Christian organizations.

Ultimately, at the end of the day and at the end of our time in leadership this is about *legacy* – what we pass on to others and what we leave behind when we move on. By legacy I am thinking specifically in terms of the raising up of new leaders who themselves will be tone-setters, culture creators and responsible stewards of places of grace, ecclesial ecosystems that exist to glorify God and to nurture the life of those within them. Through our words and actions we can lead by example and seek to infuse the next generation of Christian leaders with the gospel values, practices and behaviours that will result in safe churches and safe organizations. But this takes time, effort and a proactive investment in younger leaders. If we are to leave a positive legacy in this respect, we have to be intentional about it.

In Chapter 9 we will pick up this theme of handing the baton on to future generations and learning to step to one side to allow others space to grow into leadership. For now maybe we should take a leaf out of the Roman Catholics' book, who – at the time of writing – have just brought together one and a half million young people in Portugal! Now that is what I call being 'intentional' about investing in young leaders, and having just bumped into dozens of them at Lisbon Airport, I for one am encouraged!

Quick recap

Spiritually abusive leadership toxifies the ecclesial ecosystem with behaviours and pseudo-scriptural messaging that discolour and contaminate the water of life. In order to prevent such scenarios from taking hold in churches and parachurch organizations, it is incumbent on Christian leaders to ensure that they themselves are spiritually healthy so that they can spiritually steward others healthily. *Ordinary* leaders must expunge unrealistic expectations about the nature of ministry so as to avoid disappointment or taking their frustrations out on others and falling into the sorts of behavioural pattern that can spiral into spiritual abuse. More constructively, such leaders can curate places of grace by embodying a series of attitudes, behaviours and actions, i.e. *reflexivity, accountability, tone-setting, creating culture, mutual responsibility* and *legacy.* In this way an *unspectacular* leadership approach leads not only to 'safe spaces' but to spiritually healthy places and ecclesial ecosystems oxygenated by divine grace.

Questions for reflection

1 What are the behaviours and attitudes that characterize spiritually abusive leadership that we are describing here as *toxic*?

2 How might a mismatch of expectations concerning ministry and the reality of church work become a formula resulting in unhealthy expressions of leadership that, if left unchecked, could evolve into patterns of spiritual abuse?

3 What steps might you take in your own context in order to ensure that it might offer a generally safe environment and a spiritually healthy 'place of grace' in which people can thrive in the grace of God?

Notes

1 Humphreys, J., 2024, *Safeguarding as Mission: Learning from Encounters with Jesus*, Cambridge: Grove, p. 22.

2 Both the IICSA report (www.iicsa.org.uk) and the Jay Review published in February 2024 and available through the Church of England website (www.churchofengland.org) pick up on the failure of church institutions – and specifically the Church of England – to respond well to abuse and particularly to abuse survivors. The acronym DARVO – 'Deny, Attack, and Reverse Victim and Offender' derives from psychology and explains how abusers seek to deflect and question the credibility of victims and/or whistleblowers but it can also be used to describe how Christian organizations or individuals within organizations have themselves responded to complaints of abuse, retraumatizing victims and exacerbating the situation.

3 Humphreys, *Safeguarding as Mission*, p. 16. This quotation comes from a discussion (pp. 15–16) in which Humphreys considers Jesus' treatment of the Rich Young Ruler in Matthew 19 where choice and agency rather than coercion and control characterize Jesus' approach.

4 The quote, referring to a General Synod discussion held in July 2017, is from Lees, J., 2018, *Self-Supporting Ministry: A Practical Guide*, London: SPCK, p. 87.

5 Occasionally the Holy Spirit may move powerfully in unexpectedly quick time, but nine times out of ten church growth is the fruit of hard work, patient prayer and a painstaking process of trial and error – ask anyone who has ever been involved in church-planting.

6 In Oakley, L. and Humphreys, J., 2019, *Escaping the Maze of Spiritual Abuse: Creating Healthy Christian Cultures*, London: SPCK, pp. 134–46: some similar concepts are found in a helpful section on the creation of a 'safer, healthier, culture', though some terms, i.e. 'legacy' are used in a different way.

9

Learning to get out of the way (caring for the future)

Healthy leadership teams will encourage and release others into positions of influence and strategic importance. Ultimately, while God calls who he wants, whenever he wants, however he wants, he wants us to work together and no one is asked to go it alone. (Marcus Throup)[1]

Jesus himself is continually calling people to him in order to enable them in ministry, generally alongside others and not in isolation ... The calling and enabling of others to share in the work of ministry should therefore not be seen as some minor part or add-on optional extra to the vocation of the ordained Christian minister and leader. (Steven Croft)[2]

In an age of octogenarian presidents and megalomaniacal despots the notion of relinquishing power, stepping aside and allowing others an opportunity to shine seems somewhat counter-cultural. Seemingly, people want to gain power. Seemingly, people want to hold on to power. In politics or big business it is unusual to see people proactively seek to *share* power. In the church and Christian organizations *showmen* leaders neither share power nor delegate, except, that is, for those menial or unwanted tasks that end up being imposed on others. The default setting of the *spectacular* leadership paradigm is self-promotion, and those ambitious figureheads who claim divine authority for themselves cannot be true mentors because they view other gifted leaders as rivals to be talked down rather than fellow disciples to be built up.

Even those in the inner circle of Jesus were tempted by the

trappings of power. In the Gospels the mother of James and John ludicrously petitions Jesus on behalf of her sons that they might occupy *high office* (Matthew 20.20–27). On another occasion, in a first-century-display of 'toxic masculinity', the disciples argue among themselves about who is the greatest (Luke 22.24–27). They are told in no uncertain terms to get over themselves! Similarly today, *status* and *standing* can be significant drivers for leaders in Christian organizations but this is not the Jesus way. Instead, in the counter-cultural logic of God's Kingdom, 'the greatest among you must become like the youngest, and the leader like one who serves' (Luke 22.26). As we step up into positions of authority in the church we need to be conscious of the power we hold and tread carefully such that we don't trample down on others. Sure, some Christian leaders will need to put aside imposter syndrome, find the courage to step up and ensure they are kind to themselves. Others, though, will need to watch out for overconfidence and the flashy temptations of celebrity culture that does leadership in isolation.

For those of us who hold office in church and church-based organizations it is all too easy to get in the way. In a characteristically probing and hard-hitting talk Rowan Williams referenced the Johannine image of Jesus as 'the door', highlighting the danger of Christian leaders inadvertently getting in the way of people who are seeking to pass through![3] Surely the very last thing we want is to become a distraction or, worse, an obstacle that prevents people – including other church leaders – coming to Jesus? And yet clericalism, narcissistic posturing and spiritual abuse all act as a pernicious barring of the way to the one who is 'the way, the truth and the life' (John 14.6). Jesus had some fairly harsh words to say about those who block the path to his life-giving presence (cf. Matthew 18.6): let the *show-men* and the purveyors of *spectacular* leadership take note!

Church leaders and individuals trusted with the *shalom* well-being of Christian communities need to learn to be alert to the deceitful whisperings of the ego. Whether these whisperings suggest that we are *not good enough* or whether they claim somehow that we are *too good*, these are internal noises that bubble up so as to drown out the voice of truth. These are invasive discordant murmurings that will distract and divert us from the pastoral task, making ministry all about me when it has to be a collaborative and collective task. In the best possible sense, if we want to bring people to Jesus we will find that at times *we ourselves* need simply to step aside and get out of the way. In practice that means taking a rounded, grounded view of our individual role within the greater scheme of things that is the Kingdom of God and ensuring that as we play our part we bring other leaders into play.

In the pastoral task, on those occasions when we are engaged in self-reflection, we must reflect on where our love for others is rooted, paying attention to our inner motivations and intentions. Thus, mindful of our earlier warnings on slipping into unhealthy or spiritually abusive patterns of leadership, there is a useful thread in Dietrich Bonhoeffer's classic work *Life Together*. Bonhoeffer warns of what he calls 'emotional self-centred love', a love that *desires* rather than serves.[4] Bonhoeffer contrasts this one-sided love, which seeks to control the other, with what he calls 'spiritual love', the love that is found in and comes from Christ exclusively. To build on Bonhoeffer, any love that is mere sentimentality and ultimately self-centred is a love that places the 'I' squarely in the way of the other and so obstructs the way to Jesus. In contrast, 'spiritual love' acknowledges that 'Christ stands between me and an other' with the corollary that 'I must allow them the freedom to be Christ's'.[5]

Whereas an emotional self-centred love constrains, coerces and corners the other person, blocking the way to Jesus, spiritual love releases, empowers and prays that they might meet him and encounter his grace. Healthy leadership is a leadership infused with the love that serves the other and offers guidance but – to recap something mentioned in Chapter 8 – allows people the freedom to make their own decisions and life choices. The great theologian-martyr expresses it as follows:

Emotional love lives by uncontrolled and uncontrollable dark desires; spiritual love lives in the clear light of service ordered by the *truth*. Self-centred love results in human enslavement, bondage, rigidity; spiritual love creates the *freedom* of Christians under the Word. Emotional love breeds artificial hothouse flowers; spiritual love creates the *fruits* that grow healthily under God's open sky, according to God's good pleasure in the rain and storm and sunshine.[6]

This metaphor of fructifying organic life, which is given the right conditions to thrive under the watchful eye of the divine gardener, has multiple resonances with Scripture. We may call to mind, for example, the verdant portrait sketched out in Psalm 1, the Parable of the Sower in Mark 4, Jesus' teaching about the vine and its branches (John 15.1–17), or Paul's words concerning the 'first fruits of the Spirit' (Romans 8.23). Part of our recognizing the power we hold as Christian leaders consists in the acknowledgement that under God our conduct and comportment can help create the conditions for saplings to take root, strengthen and grow so as to become fruit-bearing life-giving entities. But just as a plant needs sunlight and nurturing rain, so fledgling church leaders need to be given access to the light and water of life that is Christ. Whereas go-it-alone *showmen* steal the thunder of upcoming leaders, and paranoid control freaks keep them in the shade, by stepping aside *ordinary* leaders model that generous 'spiritual love' that ushers others towards the one who is the light.

Towards the courageous empowering of others

It takes courage to get out of the way. Prayerfully stepping aside to beckon others forward is an act of trust. Fifteen years ago under the mentorship of indefatigable Archdeacon Luiz Souza our team in Brazil learned how to do this as time after time we prayed over our most gifted leaders and sent them out from our cathedral church to go and plant churches in needy and abandoned places. It was always tempting to stand in the way! A good case could be made for holding on to this person or that person; after all, they were stalwarts in the church with a range of responsibilities and significant contributions … But as the Archdeacon would remind us, 'as one leader moves on, God in his faithfulness raises up others!' And this, in point of fact, was exactly what happened time after time, to the extent that an entirely new diocese was birthed with the raising up and sending out of successive waves of leaders.

Empowering others to take on responsibility within a church or Christian organization is always about prayerful risk-taking. The potential to share power and to collaboratively delegate ministry responsibility is something the Church of England looks for in those who are discerning a call to priestly ministry. Knowing how and, importantly, *when* to step aside so as to gently usher another leader into a position of greater authority and responsibility is a key leadership skill. It is, perhaps, fairly obvious that self-centred *showmen* and embittered, controlling frontmen are largely incapable of releasing others into ministry. On the other hand, it is equally clear that *ordinary* leaders who are seeking the Kingdom rather than self-glorification invest in others, taking calculated and prayerful risks on those whom the Lord raises up.

In a sense, where key leaders are concerned, the intentional move to step aside is a natural way of future-proofing within any organization. Far too often, though, younger leaders are denied the opportunity to grow because of the insecurities, anxieties and controlling tendencies of leaders who are at the helm. This isn't just the tiresome *showmen*. Any leader can fall into the trap of holding on to power, micromanaging or not releasing others. But the nurturing and empowering of younger leaders coupled with the appropriate handing on of responsibility is vital if an institution is to regenerate and renew itself for present and future generations. It is therefore damaging when an established and influential leader refuses to relinquish the reins of power or pays lip service to the notion of 'collaborative ministry'.

Thankfully there are examples of *extraordinary* Christian leaders who embody a more courageous modus operandi and can inspire us in our own ministries as *ordinary* leaders. The aforementioned Brazilian Archdeacon Souza, with whom I was privileged to serve and whose constant stepping aside led to the creation of a new diocese, went on to found an Anglican primary school in an impoverished district. A few years after he had that up and running – with several hundred children getting quality schooling and alongside a new church plant next door – he handed it on to the younger local leadership he had raised up during his time living in that community. Then, at 70 years of age, he journeyed with his wife Fatima to Guinea-Bissau in West Africa, planting a church in a place where there was zero Christian presence. And what did he do after a period of time pioneering in that context? He handed on the leadership of the growing congregation to a local Muslim convert he had mentored – a man who now serves as the pastor of that church!

Not every Christian leader is called to start up extraordinary new church projects in far-flung places but every *ordinary* leader knows that ministry is never the solo act of a one-man-band. Wherever we serve and whatever the context, *unspectacular* leadership seeks to make space for younger and/or more inex-perienced leaders. Taking the time today to invest in those who will take the work forward tomorrow should be a vocational priority of every person called into ministry. Sometimes this is about opening our eyes to what God might be doing in the hearts and minds of people in our congregation or members of our team. Sometimes this is about permission-giving and encouraging a new leader to give something a go, providing the support they need and allowing them to make mistakes (after all, this is chiefly how all of us learn!).

The one caveat I would want to add here concerns diversity and the spiritual foresight that recognizes the multicoloured and pluriform nature of gifting and leadership potential. Too often in church circles the cookie-cutter principle is applied to vocational discernment processes. On those occasions when egotistical celebrity leaders appoint a sidekick they tend to go for a sort of *clone* of themselves (though being careful to ensure that the sidekick knows their place). That said, we can all be guilty of envisaging, and envisioning leadership in our own image. This is something we need to watch out for. Since we all know that team ministry is most effective when members bring complementary skill sets and giftings, we ought to be on the lookout for those who offer different leadership styles and bring giftings to the table that are different from our own.

A final word to theological educators and teachers

In a retreat house somewhere between Portsmouth and South-ampton there is a clever art graphic that portrays the word 'teaching' merging into the word 'learning' scribed directly below it but upside down. The graphic appears to suggest that 'teaching' is reflected by 'learning' and as someone who has been involved with theological education for over 20 years in various cultures I find myself drawn to this image. This, in theory and in an ideal world, is how I think things should work. Effective teaching merges seamlessly into learning and the latter is the true reflection of the former. But there is also something unsettling about the artwork.

The issue, for me at least, is that this image with its subtle messaging actually exposes much of how we go about our theological education. Many of us were brought up on the traditional university lecture model and – rather ironically – have gone on to embrace that model somewhat uncritically. The lecture room is traditionally a forum for exposition and a handy place for scholars to test out theories and new ideas on bright-eyed students. While there can be value in listening to an expert speaker expound 'their subject', the lecture format inevitably focuses attention on the teacher and their teaching. And where the lecture is largely a monologue and a one-way thing as opposed to a conversation, there can be no guarantee whatsoever that this 'teaching' translates into learning – par-ticularly where students are newcomers to academic study and to theology.

I suspect that much of our teaching falls short because it is insufficiently concerned with the flip side, that is the learning. So much of *our teaching* can be just that. It revolves around *our* agendas, *our* academic hobbyhorses, *our* scholarly fads, *our* latest theories. Now this may not be a bad thing per se but it strikes me that if in the context of theological colleges we are talking about ministerial formation then priority needs to be given to the *learning* aspect. Thus, the question is not so much 'what do we hope to teach in this session?', but 'what do we hope our students might learn and take away from this session?' Once more, we need to learn to get out of the way, forcefully pushing our personal predilections and pet projects to one side so as to take a student-centred approach.

Woe to us, then, if we overlook the *learning*. Just like a cerebral and over-intellectual sermon (cf. Chapter 6), the word-perfect lecture pregnant with technical terminology might ultimately turn out to be a meaningless monologue and a gigantic waste of time! When the people sitting in the classroom experience the polished prose of the professor as a load of Latinate gibberish, it is improbable that much 'learning' is taking place. And since we are concerned with spiritual matters, matters that are close to the heart of God, it *matters* if the lesson flies right over the students' heads. Any so-called 'teaching' that confines itself by its language and methodology to the upper echelons of incomprehensibility is most unlikely to be taken to heart.

Student-focused, learning-orientated teaching involves an invitation to those in the room to actively participate and engage. Such learning seeks to draw on the experience and knowledge that students already possess as well as identifying any gaps in knowledge and explaining terminology rather than assuming it. Engaging students at the right level in language they will understand has to take precedence: the scripted points that the teacher intends to cover can then be conveyed accordingly. Instead of a monologue, learning-orientated teaching has to be about transformational dialogue. Instead of a soliloquy, learning-orientated teaching must be an ongoing conversation. This may seem risky to more old-school educators, but these are risks we have to take.

Whether we are talking about postgraduate students getting to grips with the complexities of theology in the lecture room or small children in the Sunday class, I the *teacher* must step aside so as to invite others forward to engage in the learning space. I must feature less that they may feature more. In so doing, as a Christian teacher and leader I recognize (to recall Bonhoeffer) that a form of 'spiritual love' needs to flow through the class-room, just as it should flow through every sphere of church life. Maybe, then, this is about avoiding the temptation to become a *showman* lecturer and committing to live out a vocation as an *ordinary* teacher with an *unspectacular* teaching ministry? Perhaps. But that is most probably a conversation for another day and – I daresay – the subject of another book!

Quick recap

Spiritually abusive leadership tends to centralize and control and can block the way to Jesus. In its indisposition to dele-gate, such unhealthy leadership actively disempowers others. When *showmen* leaders stifle other leaders and prevent them from exercising their gifts, they stand in the way of the one who is 'the way, the truth and the life' (John 14.6). *Ordinary* leaders must beware of deceptive inner whisperings, whether these be negative noises that eat away at self-acceptance and self-confidence or sounds that hyperinflate the ego. In their exercise of *unspectacular* leadership such leaders will have a rounded and grounded view of themselves and will pursue a style of ministry that encourages, enables and empowers others. This tallies with the freeing 'spiritual love' that Bonhoeffer con-trasts with a controlling 'emotional self-centred love'. *Ordinary* leaders who exercise 'spiritual love' provide the conditions for other leaders to grow and bear fruit in their ministries. At times stepping back to allow others to take a lead takes courage, but missional vitality and the future-proofing of organizations depend on the type of prayerful risk-taking that releases others. A similar logic may be applied to theological education and Christian teachers, where the priority of *learning* must dictate the shape and methodology of our *teaching*.

Questions for reflection

1   What do we mean by 'learning to get out of the way' and why is this something that *ordinary* leaders should seek to do?

2   What do you make of Bonhoeffer's contrast between 'emotional self-centred love' and so-called 'spiritual love' and in what ways can we test our underlying motivations and intentions to ensure that we model healthy leadership in accordance with the gospel of grace?

3   If you are involved in teaching or leading within church or in a parachurch organization, how effective is your teaching and what might you do to *step aside* so as to enhance the learning experience of others?

Notes

1 Throup, M., 2018, *All Things Anglican*, Norwich: Canterbury Press, p. 92.

2 Croft, S., 1999, *Ministry in Three Dimensions*, London: Darton, Longman and Todd, p. 166.

3 Rowan Williams in a seminar given at the HTB Leadership Conference, London, in May 2023.

4 Kelly, G. B., ed., 2005, Daniel W. Bloesch and James H. Burtness, trans., *Life Together and Prayerbook of the Bible: Dietrich Bonhoeffer Works, Vol. 5.*, Minneapolis, MN: Fortress Press, pp. 43–5.

5 Ibid, pp. 43–4.

6 Ibid, p. 44. A possible critique of Bonhoeffer's terminology here might be that the contrasting of 'emotional love' and 'spiritual love' risks playing down or undervaluing the more positive aspects of human emotionality and disconnecting the idea of 'the spiritual' from emotionality. Notwithstanding, taken in context it is, I think, clear what Bonhoeffer is saying and he seems to be taking aim at a misplaced sentimental love of the self rather than at human emotionality.

Bibliography

Aisthorpe, S., 2020, *Rewilding the Church*, Edinburgh: St Andrew Press.

Anglican Consultative Council, The, 2019, *The Anglican Communion Safe Church Commission (ACSCC): Guidelines to Enhance the Safety of all Persons – Especially Children, Young People and Vulnerable Adults – Within the Provinces of the Anglican Communion*, London: www.anglicancommunion.org.

Barbosa, R., 2012, *Identidade Perdida*, Curitiba: Encontro.

Barron, R., 2021, *The Strangest Way: Walking the Christian Path*, Parkridge, IL: Word on Fire.

Baxter, R., 1979, *The Reformed Pastor*, Edinburgh: The Banner of Truth Trust.

Beeson, T., 2002, *The Bishops*, London: SCM.

Blue, K., 1993, *Healing Spiritual Abuse*, Downers Grove, IL: Inter-Varsity Press .

Bonhoeffer, D., 1996, *The Cost of Discipleship*, London: SCM.

Bretherton, L., 2023, *A Primer in Christian Ethics: Christ and the Struggle to Live Well*, Cambridge: Cambridge University Press.

Collicutt, J., 2015, *The Psychology of Christian Character Formation*, London: SCM.

Comer, J. M., 2019, *The Ruthless Elimination of Hurry: How to Stay Emotionally Healthy and Spiritually Alive in the Chaos of the Modern World*, London: Hodder and Stoughton.

Croft, S., 1999, *Ministry in Three Dimensions*, London: Darton, Longman and Todd.

Cuff, S., 2022, *Priesthood for all Believers: Clericalism and How to Avoid It*, London: SCM.

DeGroat, C., 2020, *When Narcissism Comes to Church: Healing Your Community from Emotional and Spiritual Abuse*, Downers Grove, IL: InterVarsity Press.

Demasure, K., 2022, 'The loss of the self – spiritual abuse of adults in the context of the Catholic church', *Religions* 13(509).

Dulles, A., 2002, *Models of the Church*, New York: Image.

Dykstra, R. C., ed., 2005, *Images of Pastoral Care: Classic Readings*, St Louis, MO: Chalice Press.

Fernandez, S., 2022, 'Victims are not guilty! Spiritual abuse and ecclesiastical responsibility', *Religions* 14(427).

Grosch Miller, C. A., 2021, *Trauma and Pastoral Care: A Ministry Handbook*, Norwich: Canterbury Press.

Harrison, J. and Innes, R., eds, 2016, *Clergy in a Complex Age: Responses to the Guidelines for the Professional Conduct of the Clergy*, London: SPCK.

Honeysett, M., 2022, *Powerful Leaders? When Church Leadership Goes Wrong and How to Prevent It*, London: InterVarsity Press.

Howard, R., 1996, *The Rise and Fall of the Nine O'Clock Service*, London: Mowbray.

Humphreys, J., 2024, *Safeguarding as Mission: Learning from Encounters with Jesus*, Cambridge: Grove.

Independent Inquiry into Child Sexual Abuse, The, 2022, www.iicsa.org.uk.

Ineson, E., 2019, *Ambition: What Jesus Said About Power, Success and Counting Stuff*, London: SPCK.

Janssens, M-L. and Corre, M., 2017, *Le Silence de la Vierge. Abus Spirituels, Derives Sectaires: Une Ancienne Religieus Temoigne*, Paris: Bayard.

Jay Review, The, 2024, www.churchofengland.org.

Johnson, D. and VanVonderen, J., 1991, *The Subtle Power of Spiritual Abuse*, Minneapolis, MN: Bethany House.

Kärkkäinnen, V-M., 2002, *An Introduction to Ecclesiology*, Downers Grove, IL: InterVarsity Press.

Kelly, E., 2012, *Personhood and Presence: Self as a Resource for Spiritual and Pastoral Care*, New York: Bloomsbury.

Kelly, G. B., ed., 2005, Daniel W. Bloesch and James H. Burtness, trans., *Life Together and Prayerbook of the Bible: Dietrich Bonhoeffer Works, Vol. 5*, Minneapolis, MN: Fortress Press.

Koyama, K., 1979, *Three Mile an Hour God*, London: SCM.

Lambeth Call on Safe Church document, The, 2023, www.anglicancommunion.org.

Lees, J., 2018, *Self-supporting Ministry: A Practical Guide*, London: SPCK.

Lewis-Anthony, J., 2009, *If You Meet George Herbert on the Road, Kill Him: Radically Rethinking Priestly Ministry*, London: Mowbray.

McIntosh, G. L. and Rima, D., 1997, *Overcoming the Dark Side of Leadership: The Paradox of Personal Dysfunction*, Grand Rapids, MI: Baker.

Morris, L., 1988, *Luke*, Leicester: InterVarsity Press.

Newman, J. H. and Neale, J. M., trans., 1957, *The Private Prayers of Lancelot Andrewes*, London: SCM.

Oakley, L. and Humphreys, J., 2019, *Escaping the Maze of Spiritual Abuse: Creating Healthy Christian Cultures*, London: SPCK.

Ortega y Gasset, J., 1988, *Notas de Andar y Ver: Viajes, Gentes e Paises*, Madrid: Alianza Editorial.

Peterson, E. H., 1989, *The Contemplative Pastor*, Dallas, TX: Word.

Poole, E., 2017, *Leadersmithing: Revealing the Trade Secrets of Leadership*, New York: Bloomsbury.

Poujol, J., 2015, *Abus Spirituels*, Paris: Empreinte.

Qualities for Ordained Ministry, The (IME 2), www.churchofengland.org.

Scarlata, M., 2019, *Sabbath Rest: The Beauty of God's Rhythm for a Digital Age*, London: SCM.

Scazzero, P., 2015, *The Emotionally Healthy Leader*, Grand Rapids, MI: Zondervan.

Spurgeon, C. H., 1960, *An All-Round Ministry*, London: The Banner of Truth Trust.

Stirling, M. and Meynell, M., eds, 2023, *Not So With You: Power and Leadership for the Church*, Eugene, OR: Wipf and Stock.

Swann, P., 2018, *Sustaining Leadership*, Abingdon: The Bible Reading Fellowship.

Thomas, R. S., 1973, *Selected Poems 1946–1968*, London: Hart-Davis, MacGibbon.

Throup, M., 2018, *All Things Anglican*, Norwich: Canterbury Press.

Throup, M., 2022, *Preaching Beyond the Pandemic*, Nottingham: Grove.

Throup, M., 2022, *When Jesus Calls*, Norwich: Canterbury Press.

Tomlin, G., 2014, *The Widening Circle*, London: SPCK.

Trible, J. L., Sr, 2005, *Transformative Pastoral Leadership in the Black Church*, New York: Palgrave Macmillan.

Walker, S. P., 2010, *The Undefended Leader*, Carlisle: Piquant.

Wilkinson, D., 2002, *The Message of Creation*, Nottingham: Inter-Varsity Press.

Williams, J., 2020, *Ecclesianarchy*, London: SCM.

Williams, R., 2003, *Silence and Honeycakes: The Wisdom of the Desert*, Oxford: Lion.

Willows, D. and Swinton, J., eds, 2000, *Spiritual Dimensions of Pastoral Care: Practical Theology in a Multidisciplinary Context*, London: Jessica Kingsley.